The

AMERICAN FOOTBALL ALMANAC

The Official Handbook of the History and Records of the National Football League

Beau Riffenburgh & Ken Thomas

G000123955

LOCHAR PUBLISHING•MOFFAT•SCOTLAND

© Beau Riffenburgh & Ken Thomas, 1991
Published by Lochar Publishing Ltd
MOFFAT DG10 9ED

British Library Cataloguing in Publication Data
Riffenburgh, Beau
The American Football almanac.
I. Title   II. Thomas, Ken
796.332

ISBN 0–948403–40–3

Typeset in 8 on 8½pt Times by Chapterhouse,
Formby L37 3PX
and printed in Scotland by Eagle Colourbooks

Publisher's Note
All information given in the following pages was correct at
the time of printing.

CONTENTS

__ACKNOWLEDGEMENTS__

The authors should like to tender their grateful thanks to Chuck Garrity, Jr. and Paul Spinelli of National Football League Properties for their assistance in obtaining information and photographs. We also wish to thank Janie and Liz, because they both deserve it.

A HISTORY OF AMERICAN FOOTBALL

THE DEVELOPMENTS OF TWELVE DECADES

Although American football is viewed as a sport that the United States is now rapidly exporting to the rest of the world, its origins are traced back to two games popular world-wide: association football (or soccer) and rugby.

In the middle of the nineteenth century, soccer and rugby were both played throughout the United States. On 6 November 1869, Rutgers and Princeton, two small colleges in New Jersey, played what is officially considered the first American football game, although its rules were much more like those of soccer than of modern American football. Each team had 25 players, and the ball could not be touched with the hands. Rutgers won six goals to four, although Princeton won a rematch eight goals to none.

In the following two decades, American football began to develop the rules that made it a new and exciting game. Many of these came from the fertile mind of Walter Camp of Yale University, a man known today as 'the father of American football'. Under Camp's guidance, the number of players per team was decreased to 11; the scrum was replaced as a manner of putting the ball in play by the center snapping the ball to the quarterback; a team was required to gain five yards in three plays (later 10 yards in four plays) in order to maintain possession of the ball; point values for touchdowns, field goals, points after touchdown, and safeties were established; and referees and penalties became a part of the game.

Red Grange, NFL Photos.

This new style of football became popular not only on college campuses, but in social or athletic clubs, where members competed on friendly (and not-so-friendly) terms with other similar clubs. A bitter rivalry developed between two of these clubs in the area of Pittsburgh, Pennsylvania – the Allegheny Athletic Association (AAA) and the Pittsburgh Athletic Club (PAC). In 1892, this rivalry resulted in the first acknowledged professional football player, when the AAA paid $500 to William (Pudge) Heffelfinger, a former three-time All-America guard at Yale, to play for them against the PAC. Heffelfinger accounted for the only score of the 4–0 game when he caused a fumble, picked up the ball, and lumbered 35 yards for a touchdown.

The hiring of a professional caused a furor, but it also established a trend that would become increasingly popular. The next year, Grant Dibert signed the first known pro football contract, when he agreed to play with the PAC for a full season, and the AAA hired the first full-time pro coach, Ben (Sport) Donnelly. By 1896, the AAA was fielding the first entirely professional team.

In the early years of the twentieth century, there were many changes in football, including the legalization of the forward pass, the requirement that seven players be on the line of scrimmage, and the reassessment of point values for touchdowns and field goals. At the same time, the center of professional football moved from western Pennsylvania to eastern Ohio, and particularly to the rival cities of Canton and Massillon. For about 15 years, the best football players in the country played in Ohio, representing teams that formed a loose, unofficial organization known as the Ohio League. In the years immediately prior to 1920, the best of these teams as often as not was the Canton Bulldogs, led by Jim Thorpe, an American Indian usually considered both the greatest football player ever and the greatest overall athlete in American history. (Thorpe also played professional baseball and won gold medals in both the decathlon and pentathlon at the 1912 Olympics in Stockholm, where King Gustav V of Sweden told him, 'Sir, you are the greatest athlete in the world'.)

But the Ohio League had definite problems. Players jumped from one team to another, depending on who was offering the most money, leading to a continual rise in salaries. There were no scheduling rules, so some teams played much harder opponents. And some teams hired players who were still in college, thereby tainting professional football with the charge of ruining the pure, amateur standing of fine young men.

On 20 August 1920, the representatives of four Ohio teams – the Canton Bulldogs, the Akron Pros, the Dayton Triangles, and the Cleveland Indians – met in Canton to

Bobby Layne, Pro Football Hall of Fame/NFL Photos.

confront the problems they faced. The result was the
founding of the American Professional Football
Association (APFA).

By the beginning of the 1920 season, the APFA had 14
teams, including ones from Ohio, Wisconsin, Indiana,
and Illinois. In the first APFA game ever played, the
Dayton Triangles defeated the Columbus Pandhandles
14–0; Lou Partlow of Dayton ran seven yards to score the
first touchdown in APFA history.

The early 1920s was a hard time for the new league, as
teams regularly were formed and then went under. But
within several years the basis for a strong organization
began to develop. In 1921, the league received a firm
guiding hand when Joe Carr was named President. He
established a league constitution and by-laws, gave teams
territorial rights, established a league office, issued the first
official standings so that there would be an undisputed
champion, forbade the signing of players who still had
college eligibility, and helped develop competitive
schedules. And in 1922, he changed the name of the
APFA, making it the National Football League.

If there was one man who could rival the importance of
Joe Carr to the NFL, it was George Halas. Halas started
off as the end, coach, and manager of the Decatur Staleys,
a team representing the A. E. Staley Manufacturing
Company. But in 1921, he became the owner of the Staleys
and moved them to Chicago, where they won the league
title. The next year Halas changed his team's name to the
Bears. In 1925, immediately upon the close of the college
football season, but while the pros were still playing, Halas
signed Harold (Red) Grange to a contract. Grange, a
halfback from the University of Illinois, was the nation's

Jim Otto, Richard Raphael/NFL Photos.

most celebrated football player. Halas used him as his
showpiece as the Bears went on two national tours as soon
as the NFL season ended, playing teams from Boston to
Los Angeles. The result was a huge increase in interest in
professional football.

In 1932, the pro game received another boost. That year,
for the first time, two teams tied for the best record in the
NFL. In order to determine a champion, those teams – the
Bears and the Portsmouth Spartans – played a
championship game in Chicago, which the Bears won 9–0.
This game so pleased the NFL owners that they made it a
regular feature of their sport, and divided the league into
two divisions, the champions of which would play for the
NFL title each year. In 1933 the NFL, which had long
followed the rules of college football, also made a number
of significant rules changes opening up play and increasing
the effect of the passing game.

In 1940 Halas's Bears made another significant
contribution. For years, the Bears had used the T-
formation, where the center snapped the ball directly into
the hands of the quarterback, rather than the more
popular Single-wing, where the tailback stood some five
yards behind the center, much as a punter does today.
When Chicago destroyed Washington 73–0 in the 1940
NFL Championship Game, the rest of the teams began to
follow the Bears' lead, and the T became the dominant
offensive formation, as it still remains today.

In 1946, the NFL received its first serious competition,
with the founding of the All-America Football
Conference, which consisted of eight teams and played an
exciting, wide-open brand of football. But unfortunately
for the AAFC, the Cleveland Browns so dominated the
league that the season ultimately became meaningless.

After four consecutive titles by the Browns, the AAFC folded, and the Browns, the San Francisco 49ers, and the Baltimore Colts joined the NFL.

The Browns, with the magnificent Otto Graham at quarterback, dominated the NFL in the 1950s, if not quite as much as they had the AAFC. They played in the NFL title game seven times in their first eight years. The teams that the Browns most often faced for the championship were the Detroit Lions and the Los Angeles Rams. The Rams were a team of offensive superstars, including quarterbacks Bob Waterfield and Norm Van Brocklin and receivers Elroy (Crazylegs) Hirsch and Tom Fears. The Lions were more a team based on the leadership of quarterback Bobby Layne, a hard-drinking, hard-living Texan who at the same time personified the will to win.

The 1958 NFL Championship Game, played on 28 December of that year, marked the beginning of a new era for pro football. In that game the Baltimore Colts and the New York Giants played the first sudden-death overtime title game in pro football history. The nation was transfixed, and, overnight, football became a game for huge television audiences. Television also played a major role the next year, when Lamar Hunt, a young Texan who had tried to purchase the Chicago Cardinals, founded the American Football League. Starting play in 1960, the AFL offered something no other NFL competitor ever had – a television contract to equal that of the NFL.

For six years the NFL and the AFL battled each other for fans, for television ratings, and for the best college players in the country. It was a time of superstars: fullback Jim Brown; quarterback Johnny Unitas; the first great names of the defense, Bob Lilly and Deacon Jones; and,

Dan Fouts, Peter Brouillet/NFL Photos.

for the first time, even offensive linemen, such as Oakland center Jim Otto. But such large sums were being spent that the teams were having serious financial problems. So in 1966, Hunt and Tex Schramm, the general manager of the Dallas Cowboys, worked out an arrangement whereby the two leagues would merge into one. The leagues immediately started a common draft and planned a title game between the champions – the Super Bowl. Four years later, in 1970, the two leagues completely merged into one – the National Football League, with the American and National Conferences. Three members of the 16-team NFL joined the 10 AFL teams in the new AFC: the Cleveland Browns, the Baltimore Colts, and the Pittsburgh Steelers.

Following the merger, the NFL became the most-popular sport in the United States, surpassing even the 'national pastime,' baseball. With unprecedented television coverage, football players became the heroes of the United States, men such as Dallas quarterback Roger Staubach, Los Angeles defensive tackle Merlin Olsen, Chicago linebacker Dick Butkus, and, perhaps the greatest of the 1970s, Buffalo running back O. J. Simpson.

Throughout the decades, the NFL constantly was willing to modify its rules to bring to its audience the most desirable game possible. Thus, in the late 1970s, the NFL opened up the passing game, creating an entirely new set of American heroes. The first quarterback to take advantage of the new rules was San Diego's Dan Fouts, but his successors included Washington's Joe Theismann, Miami's Dan Marino, Denver's John Elway, and, most successful of all, San Francisco's Joe Montana.

In recent years, Montana and his 49ers have dominated the NFL like the Bears of the 1940s, the Browns of the 1950s, the Packers of the 1960s, and the Steelers of the 1970s. But the 1980s are over, and, as time marches on, one can safely feel that a new dynasty is right around the corner about to catch its NFL rivals, and fans, unsuspecting.

TEAMS OF THE NATIONAL FOOTBALL LEAGUE

AFC EAST

Buffalo Bills
Indianapolis Colts
Miami Dolphins
New England Patriots
New York Jets

NFC EAST

Dallas Cowboys
New York Giants
Philadelphia Eagles
Phoenix Cardinals
Washington Redskins

AFC CENTRAL

Cincinnati Bengals
Cleveland Browns
Houston Oilers
Pittsburgh Steelers

NFC CENTRAL

Chicago Bears
Detroit Lions
Green Bay Packers
Minnesota Vikings
Tampa Bay Buccaneers

AFC WEST

Denver Broncos
Kansas City Chiefs
Los Angeles Raiders
San Diego Chargers
Seattle Seahawks

NFC WEST

Atlanta Falcons
Los Angeles Rams
New Orleans Saints
San Francisco 49ers

ATLANTA FALCONS

Address: Suwanee Road at I-85, Suwanee, Georgia 30174.
Telephone: (404) 945–1111.
Stadium: Atlanta-Fulton County Stadium.
Stadium Facts: capacity: 59, 643; playing surface: Grass (PAT).
Record Attendance: 60,022 vs. Dallas, 4 January 1981.
Record Margin of Victory: 55 (62–7) vs. New Orleans, 16 September 1973.
Record Margin of Loss: 59 (59–0) vs. L.A. Rams, 4 December 1976.
Team Colors: Red, Black, White, and Silver.
Chairman of the Board: Rankin M. Smith, Sr.
Head Coach: Jerry Glanville.
Some Notable Falcons: William Andrews, Steve Bartkowski, Claude Humphrey, Mike Kenn, Tommy Nobis, Gerald Riggs, R. C. Thielemann, Jeff Van Note.

Falcons Coaching History:

1966–68	Norb Hecker	4–	26–	1
1968–74	Norm Van Brocklin	37–	49–	3
1974–76	Marion Campbell	6–	19–	0
1976	Pat Peppler	3–	6–	0
1977–82	Leeman Bennett	47–	44–	0
1983–86	Dan Henning	22–	41–	1
1987–89	Marion Campbell	11–	32–	0
1989	Jim Hanifan	0–	4–	0
1990	Jerry Glanville	5–	11–	0

Titles: 1980 (NFC West).

History: The Falcons joined the NFL in 1966, as the
league's fifteenth team. They had their first winning season
(7-6-1) in 1971, but did not make the playoffs until 1978,
when they were a wild card qualifier; that year they earned
their only playoff victory ever, when they beat
Philadelphia 14-13 with two touchdown passes in the final
five minutes of the game. It is generally conceded that the
Falcons' greatest player was linebacker Tommy Nobis,
who was also their first draft selection ever, and the first
pick of the entire 1966 draft. In 1980, the Falcons won their
only AFC West title by winning a club-record nine games
in a row, to finish with a 12-4 record. Atlanta has not had a
winning record since the strike-shortened season of 1982.

Did You Know?: In 1966, both the Falcons of the NFL
and the Houston Oilers of the AFL desperately wanted
to sign Tommy Nobis, the University of Texas
linebacker, who was considered the best college football
player in America. That summer, astronaut Frank
Borman broadcast his view from outer space: 'Tell
Nobis to sign with the Oilers.'

BUFFALO BILLS

Address: One Bills Drive, Orchard Park, New York 14127.
Telephone: (716) 648–1800.
Stadium: Rich Stadium.
Stadium Facts: capacity: 80,290; playing surface:
AstroTurf.
Record Attendance: 80,208 vs. Miami 29 October 1989.
Record Margin of Victory: 48 (51–3) vs. L.A. Raiders, 20
January 1991 (AFC Championship Game).
Record Margin of Loss: 43 (43–0) vs. Baltimore, 10
October 1971.
Team Colors: Royal Blue, Scarlet Red, and White.
President: Ralph C. Wilson, Jr.
Head Coach: Marv Levy.
Some Notable Bills: Joe Ferguson, Cookie Gilchrist, Jack
Kemp, Reggie McKenzie, Billy Shaw, Fred Smerlas, Bruce
Smith, Thurman Thomas.

Bills Coaching History:

1960–61	Buster Ramsey	11–	16–	1
1962–65	Lou Saban	38–	18–	3
1966–68	Joe Collier	13–	17–	1
1968	Harvey Johnson	1–	10–	1
1969–70	Johnny Rauch	7–	20–	1
1971	Harvey Johnson	1–	13–	0
1972–76	Lou Saban	32–	29–	1
1976–77	Jim Ringo	3–	20–	0
1978–82	Chuck Knox	38–	38–	0
1983–85	Kay Stephenson	10–	26–	0
1985–86	Hank Bullough	4–	17–	0
1986–90	Marv Levy	46–	30–	0

Titles: 1964 (AFL), 1965 (AFL), 1966 (AFL East), 1980 (AFC East), 1988 (AFC East), 1989 (AFC East), 1990 (AFC).

History: In 1959, the Bills were the seventh team selected to play the next year in the first season of the American Football League. They took their names from the Buffalo football team that had been a member of the All-America Football Conference from 1947 to 1949. Buffalo running back Cookie Gilchrist became the first AFL player to rush for 1,000 yards in a season in 1962. The Bills won back-to-back championships in 1964 and 1965, but were beaten by Kansas City in the 1966 AFL Championship Game for the right to play Green Bay in the first Super Bowl. In the early and mid-1970s Buffalo was one of the greatest running teams of all time, as O. J. Simpson became the first player to rush for 2,000 yards in a season and the Bills the first team to rush for 3,000 yards.

Did You Know?: Former Buffalo quarterback Jack Kemp was one of the top contenders for the Republican Party's nomination for U.S. President in 1988. He now serves in President Bush's cabinet.

CHICAGO BEARS

Address: Halas Hall, 250 N. Washington, Lake Forest, Illinois 60045.
Telephone: (708) 295–6600.
Stadium: Soldier Field.
Stadium Facts: capacity: 66, 946; playing surface: Grass.
Record Attendance: 66,475 vs. Minnesota, 17 September 1989.
Record Margin of Victory: 73–0 vs. Washington, 8 December 1940 (NFL Championship Game).
Record Margin of Loss: 52–0 vs. Baltimore, 27 September 1964.
Team Colors: Navy Blue, Orange, and White.
Chairman of the Board: Edward W. McCaskey.
Head Coach: Mike Ditka.
Some Notable Bears: Rick Casares, Beattie Feathers, Dan Hampton, Bill McColl, Johnny Morris, Bill Osmanski, Walter Payton, Mike Singletary.

Bears Coaching History:

1920–29 George Halas	84–	31–19
1930–32 Ralph Jones	24–	10– 7
1933–42 George Halas	89–	24– 4
1942–45 Hunk Anderson–Luke Johnson	23–	12– 2
1946–55 George Halas	76–	43– 2
1956–57 John (Paddy) Driscoll	14–	10– 1
1958–67 George Halas	76–	53– 6
1968–71 Jim Dooley	20–	36– 0
1972–74 Abe Gibron	11–	30– 1
1975–77 Jack Pardee	20–	23– 0
1978–81 Neill Armstrong	30–	35– 0
1982–90 Mike Ditka	96–	51– 0

Titles: 1921 (NFL), 1932 (NFL), 1933 (NFL), 1934 (NFL West), 1937 (NFL West), 1940 (NFL), 1941 (NFL), 1942 (NFL West), 1943 (NFL), 1946 (NFL), 1956 (NFL West), 1963 (NFL), 1984 (NFC Central), 1985 (Super Bowl XX), 1986 (NFC Central), 1987 (NFC Central), 1988 (NFC Central), 1990 (NFC Central).

History: Originally known as the Decatur Staleys, the Bears were one of the founding members of the NFL in 1920, when they were a company team for the A. E. Staley Manufacturing Company. The next year, George Halas – the Staleys' manager, coach, and end – took over the ownership of the team and moved it to Chicago, where in 1922 he changed the name to the Bears. In 1932, Chicago won the first NFL Championship Game 9–0 over the Portsmouth Spartans. The Bears were one of the first teams to use the T-formation that all offenses use today, and they popularized it when they destroyed the Washington Redskins 73–0 in the 1940 NFL title game. From 1975 to 1987, the star of the Bears was Walter Payton, the leading rusher in the history of pro football, as well as the Bears' career scoring and receiving leader.

Did You Know?: Mike Ditka, the Bears' head coach, was the first tight end ever inducted into the Pro Football Hall of Fame, and is still considered the best ever at his position.

CINCINNATI BENGALS

Address: 200 Riverfront Stadium, Cincinnati, Ohio 45202.
Telephone: (513) 621–3550.
Stadium: Riverfront Stadium.
Stadium Facts: capacity: 59,755; playing surface: AstroTurf-8.
Record Attendance: 60,284 vs. Miami, 17 October 1971.
Record Margin of Victory: 54 (61-7) vs. Houston, 17 December 1989.
Record Margin of Loss: 37 (44-7) vs. Chicago, 28 September 1986.
Team Colors: Black, Orange, and White.
President: John Sawyer.
Head Coach: Sam Wyche.
Some Notable Bengals: Ken Anderson, James Brooks, Tommy Casanova, Greg Cook, Isaac Curtis, Bob Johnson, Anthony Munoz, Ken Riley, Bob Trumpy.

Bengals Coaching History:

1968–75	Paul Brown	55–	59– 1
1976–78	Bill Johnson	18–	15– 0
1978–79	Homer Rice	8–	19– 0
1980–83	Forrest Gregg	34–	27– 0
1984–90	Sam Wyche	61–	55– 0

Titles: 1970 (AFC Central), 1973 (AFC Central), 1981 (AFC), 1988 (AFC), 1990 (AFC Central).

History: The Bengals were founded in 1968, as the tenth team of the AFL. Their first head coach, and current general manager, was Paul Brown, the former great coach of Cleveland. Paul Robinson led the AFL in rushing and was named the league's rookie of the year in Cincinnati's first season. The next year, rookie quarterback Greg Cook led the AFL in passing; however, his brilliant career was cut short by a serious shoulder injury. Under Brown's tutelage, the Bengals made the playoffs in only their third season. Their quarterback through much of the 1970s and 1980s – Ken Anderson – became the first player ever to lead the NFL in passing in consecutive years two different times (1974–75 and 1981–82). The Bengals have twice played in the Super Bowl, both times being edged by San Francisco.

Did You Know?: In the 1970s, the Bengals lost two of their best defensive players ever for unusual reasons. In 1975, all-pro defensive tackle Mike Reid retired to become a concert pianist, and in 1978 all-pro defensive back Tommy Casanova retired to pursue a medical career.

CLEVELAND BROWNS

Address: Tower B, Cleveland Stadium, Cleveland, Ohio 44114.
Telephone: (216) 696-5555.
Stadium: Cleveland Stadium.
Stadium Facts: capacity: 80, 098; playing surface: Grass.
Record Attendance: 85,073 vs. N.Y. Jets, 21 September 1970.
Record Margin of Victory: 59 (62-3) vs. Washington, 7 November 1954.
Record Margin of Loss: 48 (55-7) vs. Green Bay, 12 November 1967; (51-3) vs. Minnesota, 9 November 1969.
Team Colors: Seal Brown, Orange, and White.
President and Owner: Arthur B. Modell.
Head Coach: Bill Belichick.
Some Notable Browns: Gary Collins, Doug Dieken, Gene Hickerson, Leroy Kelly, Ozzie Newsome, Mike Pruitt, Brian Sipe, Mac Speedie.

Browns Coaching History:

1946–62	Paul Brown	167– 53– 8
1963–70	Blanton Collier	79– 38– 2
1971–74	Nick Skorich	30– 26– 2
1975–77	Forrest Gregg	18– 23– 0
1977	Dick Modzelewski	0– 1– 0
1978–84	Sam Rutigliano	47– 52– 0
1984–88	Marty Schottenheimer	46– 31– 0
1989–90	Bud Carson	12– 14– 1
1990	Jim Shofner	1– 6– 0

Titles: 1946 (AAFC), 1947 (AAFC), 1948 (AAFC), 1949 (AAFC), 1950 (NFL), 1951 (NFL American Conference),

1952 (NFL American Conference), 1953 (NFL East), 1954 (NFL), 1955 (NFL), 1957 (NFL East), 1964 (NFL), 1965 (NFL East), 1967 (NFL Century Division), 1968 (NFL East), 1969 (NFL East), 1971 (AFC Central), 1980 (AFC Central), 1985 (AFC Central), 1986 (AFC Central), 1987 (AFC Central), 1989 (AFC Central).

History: The Browns were one of the original eight teams in the All-America Football Conference, a league organized to rival the NFL in 1946. Coached by Paul Brown and quarterbacked by Otto Graham, the Browns won all four AAFC titles before the league dissolved, with the Browns, the 49ers, and the Colts joining the NFL. The Browns won the NFL title their first year in the league, and were the dominant team of the 1950s. In 1956, Jim Brown joined the team and led the league in rushing eight of the next nine years. He was succeeded as the best runner in football by Leroy Kelly. In their first 28 years in pro football, the Browns had only one losing season and went to the playoffs a remarkable 21 times. This success continued in the 1980s, as Cleveland went to the playoffs seven times and played in three AFC Championship Games in four years.

Did You Know?: In his 10 years in professional football, Otto Graham led the Browns to 10 title games. They won seven league championships, and were beaten in the title game the other three times.

DALLAS COWBOYS

Address: Cowboys Center, One Cowboys Parkway, Irving, Texas 75063.
Telephone: (214) 556–9900.
Stadium: Texas Stadium.
Stadium Facts: capacity: 65,024; surface: Texas Turf.
Record Attendance: 80,259 vs. Cleveland, 24 November 1966.
Record Margin of Victory: 49 (56–7) vs. Philadelphia, 9 October 1966.
Record Margin of Loss: 44 (44–0) vs. Chicago, 17 November 1985.
Team Colors: Royal Blue, Metallic Silver Blue, and White.
Owner and President: Jerry Jones.
Head Coach: Jimmy Johnson.
Some Notable Cowboys: Tony Dorsett, Bob Hayes, Chuck Howley, Lee Roy Jordan, Don Meredith, Don Perkins, Mel Renfro, Randy White.

Cowboys Coaching History:

1960–88 Tom Landry	....	270–178–6
1989–90 Jimmy Johnson	....	8– 24– 0

Titles: 1966 (NFL East), 1967 (NFL East), 1968 (NFL Capitol Division), 1969 (NFL Capitol Division), 1970 (NFC), 1971 (Super Bowl VI), 1973 (NFC East), 1975 (NFC), 1976 (NFC East), 1977 (Super Bowl XII), 1978 (NFC), 1979 (NFC East), 1981 (NFC East), 1985 (NFC East).

History: The Cowboys joined the NFL in 1960, and its basic brain trust did not change for more than two decades: owner Clint Murchison, president/general manager Tex Schramm, personnel director Gil Brandt, and head coach Tom Landry. Although the Cowboys did not participate in the NFL draft their first year (because they joined the league too late), they still managed to obtain two star college players who would be their offensive leaders throughout the 1960s: quarterback Don Meredith and fullback Don Perkins. Landry quickly developed the most explosive offense in the NFL, and in 1966 and 1967 the Cowboys lost in the NFL Championship Game to Green Bay, for the right to play in the first two Super Bowls. Dallas was the dominant NFC team of the 1970s, going to the playoffs nine times, playing in five Super Bowls, and winning two of them. Between 1966 and 1983 the Cowboys made 17 playoff appearances in 18 years.

Did You Know?: The Cowboys lost to Green Bay 21–17 in the 1967 NFL Championship Game, which was played in a temperature of 25 degrees below zero (Celsius), with 15-mile-per-hour winds. The Packers won on a touchdown with 13 seconds left.

DENVER BRONCOS

Address: 13655 East Dove Valley Parkway, Englewood, Colorado 80112.
Telephone: (303) 649-9000.
Stadium: Denver Mile High Stadium.
Stadium Facts: capacity: 76,273; playing surface: Grass (PAT).
Record Attendance: 76,105 vs. New England, 4 January 1987 (AFC Divisional Playoff Game).
Record Margin of Victory: 43 (46–3) vs. N.Y. Jets, 19 September 1976.
Record Margin of Loss: 52 (59–7) vs. Kansas City, 7 September 1963.
Team Colors: Orange, Royal Blue, and White.
President-Chief Executive Officer: Pat Bowlen.
Head Coach: Dan Reeves.
Some Notable Broncos: John Elway, Austin (Goose) Gonsoulin, Randy Gradishar, Floyd Little, Gene Mingo, Craig Morton, Lionel Taylor, Rick Upchurch.

Broncos Coaching History:

1960–61	Frankie Filchock	7–	20– 1
1962–64	Jack Faulkner	9–	22– 1
1964–66	Mac Speedie	6–	19– 1
1966	Ray Malavasi	4–	8– 0
1967–71	Lou Saban	20–	42– 3
1971	Jerry Smith	2–	3– 0
1972–76	John Ralston	34–	33– 3
1977–80	Robert (Red) Miller	42–	25– 0
1981–90	Dan Reeves	96–	66– 1

Titles: 1977 (AFC), 1978 (AFC West), 1984 (AFC West), 1986 (AFC), 1987 (AFC), 1989 (AFC).

History: The Broncos were one of the original six teams of the American Football League. They did not have a winning season until 1973, when they went 7–5–2, and they did not go to the playoffs until 1977, when they went all the way to Super Bowl XII. The first real star of the Broncos was Lionel Taylor, a little-known end who had spent one year with the Chicago Bears. Taylor led the AFL in receiving five times in its first six years, and became the first pro football player ever to catch 100 passes in a season. Although the Broncos have lost all four times they have been in the Super Bowl, no AFC team has appeared more times in that game except the Miami Dolphins.

Did You Know?: The Broncos' sensational quarterback John Elway was the focus of one of the most important trades in franchise history. In 1983, Denver traded its number-one draft choice (guard Chris Hinton), its number-one 1984 draft pick, and quarterback Mark Hermann to Indianapolis for the rights to Elway, who was considering playing pro baseball.

DETROIT LIONS

Address: Pontiac Silverdome, 1200 Featherstone Road –
Box 4200, Pontiac, Michigan 48057.
Telephone: (313) 335-4131.
Stadium: Pontiac Silverdome.
Stadium Facts: capacity: 80,500; playing surface:
AstroTurf.
Record Attendance: 80,444 vs. Tampa Bay, 20 December
1981.
Record Margin of Victory: 45 (59–14) vs. Cleveland, 29
December 1957 (NFL Championship Game).
Record Margin of Loss: 49 (49–0) vs. Chicago Bears, 19
October 1941; and (49–0) vs. San Francisco, 1 October
1961.
Team Colors: Honolulu Blue and Silver.
President-Owner: William Clay Ford.
Head Coach: Wayne Fontes.
Some Notable Lions: Lem Barney, Roger Brown, Doug
English, Mel Farr, Alex Karras, Greg Landry, Charlie
Sanders, Billy Sims.

Lions Coaching History:

1930	Hal (Tubby) Griffin	5–	6–	3
1931–36	George (Potsy) Clark	49–	20–	6
1937–38	Earl (Dutch) Clark	14–	8–	0
1939	Elmer (Gus) Henderson	6–	5–	0
1940	George (Potsy) Clark	5–	5–	1
1941–42	Bill Edwards	4–	9–	1
1942	John Karcis	0–	8–	0
1943–47	Charles (Gus) Dorais	20–	31–	2
1948–50	Alvin (Bo) McMillin	12–	24–	0

1951–56	Raymond (Buddy) Parker	50– 24– 2
1957–64	George Wilson	55– 45– 6
1965–66	Harry Gilmer	10– 16– 2
1967–72	Joe Schmidt	43– 35– 7
1973	Don McCafferty	6– 7– 1
1974–76	Rick Forzano	15– 17– 0
1976–77	Tommy Hudspeth	11– 13– 0
1978–84	Monte Clark	43– 63– 1
1985–88	Darryl Rogers	18– 40– 0
1988–90	Wayne Fontes	15– 22– 0

Titles: 1935 (NFL), 1952 (NFL), 1953 (NFL), 1954 (NFL West), 1957 (NFL), 1983 (NFC Central).

History: The Lions were originally founded in Portsmouth, Ohio, and known as the Spartans. They did not move to Detroit until 1934, when they were purchased by George Richards, a Detroit radio station owner. The Lions were one of the dominant teams of the 1950s, with a backfield of quarterback Bobby Layne, halfbacks Doak Walker and Bob Hoernschemeyer, and fullback Pat Harder. During this period, they won three NFL titles in six years. In the late 1950s, the Lions were purchased by William Clay Ford, the grandson of Henry Ford, the founder of the Ford Motor Corporation. Through much of the 1970s, the Lions were bridesmaids in the NFC Central Division, finishing in second place seven years in a row.

Did You Know?: Doug English, the Lions' all-pro defensive tackle of the 1970s and 1980s, actually retired after the 1979 season to pursue his business interests with an oil company? After one year, English rejoined the Lions because he missed football; subsequently he was selected to the Pro Bowl three consecutive years.

GREEN BAY PACKERS

Address: 1265 Lombardi Avenue, P.O. Box 10628, Green Bay, Wisconsin 54307–0628.
Telephone: (414) 496–5700.
Stadiums: Lambeau Field; Milwaukee County Stadium.
Stadium Facts: capacity: 59,543 (Lambeau Field) and 56,051 (Milwaukee County Stadium); playing surface: Grass (both).
Record Attendance: 56,895 vs. Chicago, 3 November 1985.
Record Margin of Victory: 53 (56–3) vs. Atlanta, 23 October 1966.
Record Margin of Loss: 54 (61–7) vs. Chicago, 7 December 1980.
Team Colors: Dark Green, Gold, and White.
Chairman of the Board: Robert J. Parins.
Head Coach: Lindy Infante.
Some Notable Packers: John Brockington, Lynn Dickey, Bobby Dillon, Gale Gillingham, Cecil Isbell, Jerry Kramer, James Lofton, Dave Robinson.

Packers Coaching History:

1921–49	Earl (Curly) Lambeau	212–106–21
1950–53	Gene Ronzani	14– 31– 1
1953	Hugh Devore – Ray (Scooter) McLean	0– 2– 0
1954–57	Lisle Blackbourn	17– 31– 0
1958	Ray (Scooter) McLean	1– 10– 1
1959–67	Vince Lombardi	98– 30– 4
1968–70	Phil Bengtson	20– 21– 1
1971–74	Dan Devine	25– 28– 4

1975–83 Bart Starr	53– 77– 3
1984–87 Forrest Gregg	25– 37– 1
1988–90 Lindy Infante	20– 28– 0

Titles: 1929 (NFL), 1930 (NFL), 1931 (NFL), 1936 (NFL), 1938 (NFL West), 1939 (NFL), 1944 (NFL), 1960 (NFL West), 1961 (NFL), 1962 (NFL), 1965 (NFL), 1966 (Super Bowl I), 1967 (Super Bowl II), 1972 (NFC Central).

History: The Packers were founded in 1919 as an independent club, and named for the Indian Packing Company, which helped sponsor them. Two years later they joined the NFL. In their early years, the Packers were run by Earl (Curly) Lambeau, one of their founders, who also played halfback and served as coach, general manager, publicity man, and ticket salesman. In the 1930s, and again in the 1950s, the club was reorganized with public stock sales. It is the only community-owned team in major professional sports in America. The Packers were the dominant team in the NFL in the 1960s, under the leadership of coach Vince Lombardi. In an eight-year period, Lombardi won six conference titles, five NFL titles, and the first two Super Bowls. The Super Bowl championship trophy is named after him.

Did You Know?: In 1922 Earl (Curly) Lambeau changed the name of his team from the Packers to the Blues. However, the fans and the local media refused to accept the name change and continued to call the team the Packers. Midway through the season, Lambeau gave in to public demand and officially went back to calling the team the Packers.

HOUSTON OILERS

Address: 6910 Fannin Street, Houston, Texas 77030.
Telephone: (713) 797–9111.
Stadium: Astrodome.
Stadium Facts: capacity: 60,502; playing surface: AstroTurf-8.
Record Attendance: 60,694 vs. Cincinnati 13 November 1989.
Record Margin of Victory: 55 (55–0) vs. Oakland, 9 September 1961.
Record Margin of Loss: 54 (61–7) vs. Cincinnati, 17 December 1989.
Team Colors: Columbia Blue, Scarlet, and White.
President: K. S. (Bud) Adams, Jr.
Head Coach: Jack Pardee.
Some Notable Oilers: Elvin Bethea, Robert Brazile, Billy Cannon, Hoyle Granger, Leon Gray, Warren Moon, Mike Munchak, George Webster.

Oilers Coaching History:

1960–61	Lou Rymkus	12–	7–	1
1961	Wally Lemm	10–	0–	0
1962–63	Frank (Pop) Ivy)	17–	12–	0
1964	Sammy Baugh	4–	10–	0
1965	Hugh Taylor	4–	10–	0
1966–70	Wally Lemm	28–	40–	4
1971	Ed Hughes	4–	9–	1
1972–73	Bill Peterson	1–	18–	0
1973–74	Sid Gillman	8–	15–	0
1975–80	Bum Phillips	59–	38–	0
1981–83	Ed Biles	8–	23–	0

1983	Chuck Studley	2- 8- 0
1984–85	Hugh Campbell	8- 22- 0
1985–89	Jerry Glanville	35- 35- 0
1990	Jack Pardee	9- 8- 0

Titles: 1960 (AFL), 1961 (AFL), 1962 (AFL East), 1967 (AFL East).

History: The Oilers were one of the original six AFL teams, with a name selected, according to their owner, for 'sentimental and social reasons.' Before their first season, the Oilers made the biggest acquisition of the entire league – signing Heisman Trophy winner Billy Cannon, a halfback from Louisiana State. Cannon immediately gave a certain amount of credibility to the new league. In 1962, the Oilers became the first AFL team to sign a player still on an NFL roster, tight end Willard Dewveall of the Chicago Bears. Currently, the Oilers' offensive line is perhaps the best in pro football, headed by guards Mike Munchak and Bruce Matthews and tackle Dean Steinkuhler. The Oilers feature the most wide-open passing attack in the NFL.

Did You Know?: Pro Bowl guard Bruce Matthews is the younger brother of Cleveland's long-time Pro Bowl linebacker Clay Matthews. Both are the sons of former San Francisco defensive end Clay Matthews, Sr.

INDIANAPOLIS COLTS

Address: P.O. Box 535000, Indianapolis, Indiana 46253.
Telephone: (317) 297-2658.
Stadium: Hoosier Dome.
Stadium Facts: capacity: 60,127; playing surface: Astro-Turf.
Record Attendance: 61,479 vs. Pittsburgh, 13 November 1983.
Record Margin of Victory: 56 (56-0) vs. Green Bay, 2 November 1958.
Record Margin of Loss: 57 (57-0) vs. Chicago, 25 November 1962.
Team Colors: Royal Blue and White.
President-Treasurer: Robert Irsay.
Head Coach: Ron Meyer.
Some Notable Colts: Alan Ameche, Mike Curtis, Eric Dickerson, Chris Hinton, Bert Jones, George Kunz, Tom Matte, Lydell Mitchell.

Colts Coaching History:

1953	Keith Molesworth	3-	9- 0
1954-62	Weeb Ewbank	61-	52- 1
1963-69	Don Shula	73-	26- 4
1970-72	Don McCafferty	26-	11- 1
1972	John Sandusky	4-	5- 0
1973-74	Howard Schnellenberger	4-	13- 0
1974	Joe Thomas	2-	9- 0
1975-79	Ted Marchibroda	41-	36- 0
1980-81	Mike McCormack	9-	23- 0
1982-84	Frank Kush	11-	28- 1
1984	Hal Hunter	0-	1- 0

| 1985–86 | Rod Dowhower | 5– 24– 0 |
| 1986–90 | Ron Meyer | 36– 31– 0 |

Titles: 1958 (NLF), 1959 (NFL), 1964 (NFL West), 1968 (NFL), 1970 (Super Bowl V), 1975 (AFC East), 1976 (AFC East), 1977 (AFC East), 1987 (AFC East).

History: The Colts were originally located in Baltimore and owned by Carroll Rosenbloom. Rosenbloom was a master at selecting coaches, and gave starts to Hall of Fame coach Weeb Ewbank as well as to Don Shula, the second-winningest coach in NFL history. Led by the great Johnny Unitas at quarterback, the Colts defeated the New York Giants 23–17 in overtime for the 1958 NFL title, in a game usually considered the greatest of all time. The Colts were also the victims of the greatest upset in pro football history – their 16–7 loss to the New York Jets in Super Bowl III. In 1972 Rosenbloom traded the Colts to Robert Irsay in exchange for the Los Angeles Rams. In 1984 Irsay moved the club to Indianapolis.

Did You Know?: Don McCafferty was the first coach to win the Super Bowl in his rookie year. In 1970, he succeeded Don Shula, who had joined the Miami Dolphins, and took the Colts to the AFC East crown, the AFC championship, and a 16–13 victory over Dallas in Super Bowl V.

KANSAS CITY CHIEFS

Address: One Arrowhead Drive, Kansas City, Missouri 64129.
Telephone: (816) 924–9300.
Stadium: Arrowhead Stadium.
Stadium Facts: capacity: 78,067; playing surface: AstroTurf-8.
Record Attendance: 82,094 vs. Oakland, 5 November 1972.
Record Margin of Victory: 52 (59–7) vs. Denver, 7 September 1963.
Record Margin of Loss: 45 (45–0) vs. Pittsburgh, 7 November 1976; (45–0) vs. Seattle, 4 November 1984.
Team Colors: Red, Gold, and White.
Owners: Lamar Hunt.
Head Coach: Marty Schottenheimer.
Some Notable Chiefs: Fred Arbanas, Ed Budde, Deron Cherry, Mike Garrett, E. J. Holub, Jerry Mays, Johnny Robinson, Jim Tyrer.

Chiefs Coaching History:

1960–74	Hank Stram	129–	79–10
1975–77	Paul Wiggin	11–	24– 0
1977	Tom Bettis	1–	6– 0
1978–82	Marv Levy	31–	42– 0
1983–86	John Mackovic	30–	35– 0
1987–88	Frank Gansz	8–	22– 1
1989–90	Marty Schottenheimer	19–	13– 1

Titles: 1962 (AFL), 1966 (AFL), 1969 (Super Bowl IV), 1971 (AFC West).

History: The Chiefs were one of the six original AFL teams, when they were located in Dallas and originally known as the Texans. In fact, their owner, Lamar Hunt, was the man who came up with the idea for the founding of the AFL. Along with Tex Schramm of the Dallas Cowboys, Hunt also was most responsible for the AFL–NFL merger. Because of competition with the NFL's Cowboys, Hunt moved his team to Kansas City in 1963, the years after the Texans won the AFL title. Three years later, they were the first team to represent the AFL in the Super Bowl. In 1969, the Chiefs won Super Bowl IV, the last game between the AFL and NFL before their realignment into one league with two conferences.

Did You Know?: In 1966, the Chiefs selected Heisman Trophy winner Mike Garrett, a halfback from USC, in the twentieth round of the draft. The other AFL teams were so sure that Garrett would sign with his hometown Los Angeles Rams of the NFL that they did not want to waste a pick on him. But the Chiefs signed Garrett, and he became their season and career rushing leader.

LOS ANGELES RAIDERS

Address: 332 Center Street, El Segundo, California 90245.
Telephone: (213) 322-3451.
Stadium: Los Angeles Memorial Coliseum.
Stadium Facts: capacity: 92,488; playing surface: Grass.
Record Attendance: 90,334 vs. Pittsburgh, 1 January 1984.
Record Margin of Victory: 49 (56-7) vs. Houston, 21 December 1969 (AFL Divisional Playoff Game).
Record Margin of Loss: 55 (55-0) vs. Houston, 9 September 1961.
Team Colors: Silver and Black.
President of the Managing General Partner: Al Davis.
Head Coach: Art Shell.
Some Notable Raiders: Marcus Allen, Pete Banaszak, Ray Chester, Clem Daniels, Ben Davidson, Daryle Lamonica, Kent McCloughan, Ken Stabler.

Raiders Coaching History:

1960–61	Eddie Erdelatz	6–	10–	0
1961–62	Marty Feldman	2–	15–	0
1962	Red Conkright	1–	8–	0
1963–65	Al Davis	23–	16–	3
1966–68	Johnny Rauch	35–	10–	1
1969–78	John Madden	112–	39–	7
1979–87	Tom Flores	91–	56–	0
1988–89	Mike Shanahan	8–	12–	0
1989–90	Art Shell	20–	10–	0

Titles: 1967 (AFL), 1968 (AFL West), 1969 (AFL West), 1970 (AFC West), 1972 (AFC West), 1973 (AFC West),

1974 (AFC West), 1975 (AFC West), 1976 (Super Bowl XI), 1980 (Super Bowl XV), 1983 (Super Bowl XVIII), 1985 (AFC West), 1990 (AFC West).

History: The Raiders were one of the original AFL teams, although they were initially supposed to be located in Minneapolis. But when the NFL awarded a team to Minnesota, the new AFL franchise moved to Oakland for its first season. The Raiders were one of the best teams in pro football in the late 1960s and throughout the 1970s: between 1967 and 1976, they played in eight AFL or AFC title games. In 1982, two years after winning their second Super Bowl, the Raiders moved to the Los Angeles Memorial Coliseum, which had been vacated by the Los Angeles Rams. Two years later, they brought the only Super Bowl title to Los Angeles.

Did You Know?: The Raiders have the best record in Monday night football games of any team. In the past 21 years, they have gone 29-6-1 in Monday night contests.

LOS ANGELES RAMS

Address: 2327 West Lincoln Avenue, Anaheim, California 92801.
Telephone: (714) 535-7267.
Stadium: Anaheim Stadium.
Stadium Facts: capacity: 69,008; playing surface: Grass.
Record Attendance: 67,037 vs. N.Y. Giants, 23 December 1984 (NFC Wild Card Game).
Record Margin of Victory: 59 (59-0) vs. Atlanta, 4 December 1976.
Record Margin of Loss: 48 (48-0) vs. San Francisco, 27 December 1987.
Team Colors: Royal Blue, Gold, and White.
President: Georgia Frontiere.
Head Coach: John Robinson.
Some Notable Rams: Nolan Cromwell, Roman Gabriel, Dennis Harrah, Tom Mack, Jack Reynolds, Les Richter, Jackie Slater, Jack Youngblood.

Rams Coaching History:

1937–38	Hugo Bezdek	1– 13–	0
1938	Art Lewis	4– 4–	0
1939–42	Earl (Dutch) Clark	16– 26–	2
1944	Aldo (Buff) Donelli	4– 6–	0
1945–46	Adam Walsh	16– 5–	1
1947	Bob Snyder	6– 6–	0
1948–49	Clark Shaughnessy	14– 8–	3
1950–52	Joe Stydahar	19– 9–	0
1952–54	Hamp Pool	23– 11–	2
1955–59	Sid Gillman	28– 32–	1
1960–62	Bob Waterfield	9– 24–	1

1962–65	Harland Svare	14– 31– 3
1966–70	George Allen	49– 19– 4
1971–72	Tommy Prothro	14– 12– 2
1973–77	Chuck Knox	57– 20– 1
1978–82	Ray Malavasi	43– 36– 0
1983–90	John Robinson	76– 61– 0

Titles: 1945 (NFL), 1949 (NFL West), 1950 (NFL National Conference), 1951 (NFL), 1955 (NFL West), 1967 (NFL Coastal Division), 1969 (NFL Coastal Division), 1973 (NFC West), 1974 (NFC West), 1975 (NFC West), 1976 (NFC West), 1977 (NFC West), 1978 (NFC West), 1979 (NFC), 1985 (NFC West).

History: The Rams were founded in 1937 in Cleveland, Ohio. Homer Marshman, the original owner, sold the Rams to Daniel F. Reeves and Fred Levy in 1941. The club suspended operations for one year (1943) during World War II, but came back two years later to win the NFL title. The next years Reeves moved his club to Los Angeles, where it became the first NFL team located on the west coast. During the early 1950s, the Rams were loaded with talent, and many experts still think they were the best offensive club ever assembled. The Rams have always been known for their innovative coaches, including Clark Shaughnessy, Hamp Pool, Sid Gillman, and George Allen. They have had one of the greatest – and most successful coaches in each of the last three decades: Allen in the 1960s, Chuck Knox in the 1970s, and John Robinson in the 1980s.

Did You Know?: In the late 1940s and early 1950s, the Rams had the unusual distinction of having *two* Hall of Fame quarterbacks on the same team: Bob Waterfield and Norm Van Brocklin. Waterfield led the NFL in passing in 1946 and 1951, and Van Brocklin did the same in 1950, 1952, and 1954.

MIAMI DOLPHINS

Address: Joe Robbie Stadium, 2269 N.W. 199th Street, Miami, Florida 33056.
Telephone: (305) 620–5000.
Stadium: Joe Robbie Stadium.
Stadium Facts: capacity: 73,000; playing surface: Grass (PAT).
Record Attendance: 68,292 vs. N.Y. Jets, 23 October 1988.
Record Margin of Victory: 52 (52–0) vs. New England, 12 November 1972.
Record Margin of Loss: 45 (48–3) vs. Kansas City, 28 September 1968.
Team Colors: Aqua, Coral, and White.
President: Timothy J. Robbie.
Head Coach: Don Shula.
Some Notable Dolphins: Dick Anderson, Jim Kiick, Bob Kuechenberg, Larry Little, Dan Marino, Eugene (Mercury) Morris, Jake Scott, Dwight Stephenson.

Dolphins Coaching History:

1966–69 George Wilson	....	15– 39– 1
1970–90 Don Shula	....	225–111– 2

Titles: 1971 (AFC), 1972 (Super Bowl VII), 1973 (Super Bowl VIII), 1974 (AFC East), 1979 (AFC East), 1981 (AFC East), 1982 (AFC), 1983 (AFC East), 1984 (AFC), 1985 (AFC East).

History: The Dolphins were formed in 1966 as the ninth member of the American Football League. Although they did not win very often their first several years, they built the nucleus of a strong team, drafting such players as quarterback Bob Griese, fullback Larry Csonka, and halfback Jim Kiick. In 1970 Don Shula became the Dolphins head coach and immediately turned the team around. In Shula's first year Miami improved from a 3-10-1 record to 10-4 and a wild-card playoff berth. The next year they were in the Super Bowl. And the next year they became the only NFL team ever to establish a perfect regular and post-season record. The Dolphins are among the best-coached team in the NFL, and they lead the league in fewest penalties almost every year.

> ***Did You Know?***: The Dolphins got off to an auspicious start. In their first regular season game ever, halfback Joe Auer took the opening kickoff – the first time a Dolphins player had ever touched the ball – and returned it for a touchdown against the Oakland Raiders. However, the Raiders won the game 23–14.

MINNESOTA VIKINGS

Address: 9520 Viking Drive, Eden Prairie, Minnesota 55344.
Telephone: (612) 828–6500.
Stadium: Hubert H. Humphrey Metrodome.
Stadium Facts: capacity: 63,000; playing surface: AstroTurf.
Record Attendance: 62,851 vs. Chicago, 19 October 1986.
Record Margin of Victory: 48 (51–3) vs. Cleveland, 9 November 1969.
Record Margin of Loss: 44 (51–7) vs. San Francisco, 8 December 1984.
Team Colors: Purple, Gold, and White.
Chairman of the Board: John Skoglund.
Head Coach: Jerry Burns.
Some Notable Vikings: Matt Blair, Bill Brown, Carl Eller, Chuck Foreman, Ahmad Rashad, Jeff Siemon, Mick Tingelhoff, Ron Yary.

Vikings Coaching History:

1961–66	Norm Van Brocklin	29–	51–	4
1967–83	Bud Grant	161–	99–	5
1984	Les Steckel	3–	13–	0
1985	Bud Grant	7–	9–	0
1986–90	Jerry Burns	47–	38–	0

Titles: 1968 (NFL Central), 1969 (NFL), 1970 (NFC Central), 1971 (NFC Central), 1973 (NFC), 1974 (NFC), 1975 (NFC Central), 1976 (NFC), 1977 (NFC Central), 1978 (NFC Central), 1980 (NFC Central), 1989 (NFC Central).

History: The Vikings were founded in 1961 as the NFL's fourteenth team. Their initial head coach was Norm Van Brocklin, who had quarterbacked Philadelphia to the NFL title just the previous season. The Vikings were not a consistent winner until Bud Grant became the head coach. In his second year, Grant took his team to the NFL Central Division title, and the next year he led them to the first of their four Super Bowls, all of which have been losses. During the late 1960s and early 1970s, the Vikings had one of the greatest defensive lines of all time, the 'Purple People Eaters', consisting of defensive ends Jim Marshall and Carl Eller and defensive tackles Alan Page and Gary Larsen. For many years, the Vikings' offensive star was quarterback Fran Tarkenton, the most productive quarterback in NFL history.

Did You Know?: Minnesota joined the NFL with a bang. In their first game, the Vikings shocked the Chicago Bears 37-13, as rookie quarterback Fran Tarkenton passed for four touchdowns and ran for another.

NEW ENGLAND PATRIOTS

Address: Foxboro Stadium, Route 1, Foxboro, Massachusetts 02035.
Telephone: (508) 543-8200.
Stadium: Foxboro Stadium.
Stadium Facts: capacity: 60,794; playing surface: Grass.
Record Attendance: 61,457 vs. Miami, 5 December 1971.
Record Margin of Victory: 53 (56-3) vs. N.Y. Jets, 9 September 1979.
Record Margin of Loss: 52 (52-0) vs. Miami, 12 November 1972.
Team Colors: Red, White, and Blue.
Chairman: Victor K. Kiam II.
Head Coach: Dick MacPherson.
Some Notable Patriots: Nick Buoniconti, Gino Cappelletti, Steve Grogan, Mike Haynes, Stanley Morgan, Jon Morris, Jim Nance, Andre Tippett.

Patriots Coaching History:

Years	Coach	W	L	T
1960-61	Lou Saban	7	12	0
1961-68	Mike Holovak	53	37	9
1969-70	Clive Rush	5	16	0
1970-72	John Mazur	9	21	0
1972	Phil Bengtson	1	4	0
1973-78	Chuck Fairbanks	46	41	0
1978	Hank Bullough–Ron Erhardt	0	1	0
1979-81	Ron Erhardt	21	27	0
1982-84	Ron Meyer	18	16	0
1984-89	Raymond Berry	51	41	0
1990	Rod Rust	1	15	0

Titles: 1963 (AFL East), 1978 (AFC East), 1985 (AFC), 1986 (AFC East).

History: The Patriots were the eighth club chosen as one of the original members of the American Football League, when they were known as the Boston Patriots. On 9 September 1960, in the first regular-season game in AFL history, the Patriots were defeated by the Denver Broncos 13–10. The Patriots' first star player was a wide receiver and kicker named Gino Cappelletti, who led the AFL in scoring five times in its first seven years. In the late 1960s the Patriots had the most effective runner in the AFL, big fullback Jim Nance, who twice led the league in rushing. After the 1985 season, the Patriots became the first team to go to the Super Bowl after having had to win three playoff games on the road; they defeated the Jets, the Raiders, and the Dolphins, before losing to the Bears in Super Bowl XX.

Did You Know?: The Patriots hold the NFL season record for most yards gained rushing by a team – 3,165 in 1978, when four backs had more than 500 yards: fullback Sam Cunningham (768), halfback Horace Ivory (693), halfback Andy Johnson (675), and quarterback Steve Grogan (539).

NEW ORLEANS SAINTS

Address: 1500 Poydras Street, New Orleans, Louisiana 70112.
Telephone: (504) 733-0255.
Stadium: Louisiana Superdome.
Stadium Facts: capacity: 69,065; playing surface: AstroTurf.
Record Attendance: 70,940 vs. Atlanta, 4 November 1979.
Record Margin of Victory: 42 (42–0) vs. Denver, 20 November 1988.
Record Margin of Loss: 55 (62–7) vs. Atlanta, 16 September 1973.
Team Colors: Old Gold, Black, and White.
Owner/General Partner: Tom Benson.
Head Coach: Jim Mora.
Some Notable Saints: Dan Abramowicz, Morten Andersen, Bruce Clark, Rickey Jackson, Archie Manning, Tommy Myers, George Rogers, Dave Whitsell.

Saints Coaching History:

Years	Coach			
1967–70	Tom Fears	13–	34–	2
1970–72	J. D. Roberts	7–	25–	3
1973–75	John North	11–	23–	0
1975	Ernie Hefferle	1–	7–	0
1976–77	Hank Stram	7–	21–	0
1978–80	Dick Nolan	15–	29–	0
1980	Dick Stanfel	1–	3–	0
1981–85	Bum Phillips	27–	42–	0
1985	Wade Phillips	1–	3–	0
1986–90	Jim Mora	46–	35–	0

Titles: None.

History: The Saints were founded in 1967, as the NFL's sixteenth team. Like the Dolphins the year before, the Saints scored on the opening kickoff of their first-ever game, with rookie John Gilliam returning the ball 94 yards for a touchdown against the Rams. Despite not having a winning record until the 1987 season, the Saints have had their share of star players. The first was split end Dan Abramowicz, who was slow and lumbering, but made himself one of the best receivers in pro football by hard work. Another was the great quarterback Archie Manning, who meant so much to the team that he was selected the NFC's most valuable player in 1978, despite the Saints going only 7–9.

Did You Know?: The Saints' team name was selected in honor of the Dixieland classic 'When the Saints Go Marchin' In,' which was one of the hits by trumpet player Al Hirt, one of the Saints' original minority owners.

NEW YORK GIANTS

Address: Giants Stadium, East Rutherford, New Jersey 07073.
Telephone: (201) 935–8111.
Stadium: Giants Stadium.
Stadium Facts: capacity: 77,152; playing surface: AstroTurf.
Record Attendance: 76,633 vs. Washington, 11 January 1987 (NFC Championship Game).
Record Margin of Victory: 56 (56–0) vs. Philadelphia, 15 October 1933.
Record Margin of Loss: 56 (63–7) vs. Pittsburgh, 30 November 1952.
Team Colors: Blue, Red, and White.
President: Wellington T. Mara.
Head Coach: Ray Handley.
Some Notable Giants: Harry Carson, Charlie Conerly, Homer Jones, Carl (Spider) Lockhart, Kyle Rote, Phil Simms, Lawrence Taylor, Brad Van Pelt.

Giants Coaching History:

1925	Bob Folwell		8–	4–	0
1926	Joe Alexander		8–	4–	1
1927–28	Earl Potteiger		15–	8–	3
1929–30	LeRoy Andrews		24–	5–	1
1930	Benny Friedman		2–	0–	0
1931–53	Steve Owen		153–	108–	17
1954–60	Jim Lee Howell		54–	29–	4
1961–68	Allie Sherman		57–	54–	4
1969–73	Alex Webster		29–	40–	1
1974–76	Bill Arnsparger		7–	28–	0

1976–78	John McVay	14– 23– 0
1979–82	Ray Perkins	24– 35– 0
1983–90	Bill Parcells	85– 52– 1

Titles: 1927 (NFL), 1933 (NFL East), 1934 (NFL), 1935 (NFL East), 1938 (NFL), 1939 (NFL East), 1941 (NFL East), 1944 (NFL East), 1946 (NFL East), 1956 (NFL), 1958 (NFL East), 1959 (NFL East), 1961 (NFL East), 1962 (NFL East), 1963 (NFL East), 1986 (Super Bowl XXI), 1989 (NFC East), 1990 (Super Bowl XXV).

History: The Giants were founded in 1925 by Tim Mara, and the family still is represented by his younger son, Wellington, who is half-owner. The Giants were not immediately successful, but the appearance of Red Grange and the Bears on 6 December 1925 drew more than 73,000 fans into the old Polo Grounds and turned a negative cash flow into a financial bonanza. The glory years for the Giants were the late 1950s and early 1960s. In 1956 they won the NFL title with a smashing 47–7 victory over the Chicago Bears. In the six years between 1958 and 1963, the Giants appeared in five NFL Championship Games, although they lost each time, twice to the Colts, twice to the Packers, and once to the Bears. After a sluggish period in the 1970s, Bill Parcells returned the Giants to the top, before retiring this past spring.

Did You Know?: In the late 1950s, the Giants had perhaps the greatest coaching staff ever assembled. The head coach was Jim Lee Howell, who took his team to three title games in a four-year period. The defensive assistant was Tom Landry, who became head coach of the Cowboys, whom he guided to five Super Bowls. And the offensive assistant was Vince Lombardi, who became head coach of the Packers, whom he led to five NFL titles.

NEW YORK JETS

Address: 1000 Fulton Avenue, Hempstead, New York 11550.
Telephone: (516) 538–6600.
Stadium: Giants Stadium.
Stadium Facts: capacity: 76,891; playing surface: AstroTurf.
Record Attendance: 74,975 vs. N.Y. Giants, 2 December 1984.
Record Margin of Victory: 42 (45–3) vs. Houston, 18 September 1988.
Record Margin of Loss: 53 (56–3) vs. New England, 9 September 1979.
Team Colors: Kelly Green and White.
Chairman of the Board: Leon Hess.
Head Coach: Bruce Coslet.
Some Notable Jets: Winston Hill, Freeman McNeil, Ken O'Brien, Marvin Powell, George Sauer, Matt Snell, Al Toon, Wesley Walker.

Jets Coaching History:

1960–61	Sammy Baugh	14–	14–	0	
1962	Clyde (Bulldog) Turner	5–	9–	0	
1963–73	Weeb Ewbank	73–	78–	6	
1974–75	Charley Winner	9–	14–	0	
1975	Ken Shipp	1–	4–	0	
1976	Lou Holtz	3–	10–	0	
1976	Mike Holovak	0–	1–	0	
1977–82	Walt Michaels	41–	49–	1	
1983–89	Joe Walton	54–	59–	1	
1990	Bruce Coslet	6–	10–	1	

Titles: 1968 (Super Bowl III), 1969 (AFL East).

History: The Jets were founded as one of the AFL's original six teams, whey they were known as the Titans, a take-off on the Giants. In 1963, the team was purchased by a syndicate that renamed it the Jets and made Weeb Ewbank the head coach. Two years later, the Jets drafted Joe Namath, who not only became the first player ever to pass for 4,000 yards in a season (in 1967), but who led the team to successive divisional titles (1968–69) and to a victory in Super Bowl III. Namath was rarely healthy for an entire season after the Super Bowl victory, and after 1969 the Jets did not make the playoffs until 1981.

Did You Know?: The first player who signed with the Titans was Don Maynard, a free agent flanker from Texas Western, who had been playing in Canada. Maynard became an immediate star, catching 72 passes for 1,265 yards his first year. He had four more 1,000-yard seasons before he retired as pro football's all-time receiving leader with 633 catches.

PHILADELPHIA EAGLES

Address: Veterans Stadium, Broad Street and Pattison Avenue, Philadelphia, Pennsylvania 19148.
Telephone: (215) 463-2500.
Stadium: Veterans Stadium.
Stadium Facts: capacity: 65,356; playing surface: AstroTurf-8.
Record Attendance: 72,111 vs. Dallas, 1 November 1981.
Record Margin of Victory: 64 (64-0) vs. Cincinnati Reds, 6 November 1934.
Record Margin of Loss: 56 (56-0) vs. N.Y. Giants, 15 October 1933.
Team Colors: Kelly Green, Silver, and White.
Owner: Norman Braman.
Head Coach: Rich Kotite.
Some Notable Eagles: Maxie Baughan, Bill Bradley, Harold Carmichael, Ron Jaworski, Tommy McDonald, Wilbert Montgomery, Mike Quick, Reggie White.

Eagles Coaching History:

1933-35	Lud Wray	9-	21- 1
1936-40	Bert Bell	10-	44- 2
1941-50	Earle (Greasy) Neale	66-	44- 5
1951	Alvin (Bo) McMillin	2-	0- 0
1951	Wayne Millner	2-	8- 0
1952-55	Jim Trimble	25-	20- 3
1956-57	Hugh Devore	7-	16- 1
1958-60	Lawrence (Buck) Shaw	20-	16- 1
1961-63	Nick Skorich	15-	24- 3
1964-68	Joe Kuharich	28-	41- 1
1969-71	Jerry Williams	7-	22- 2

1971–72	Ed Khayat	8– 15– 2
1973–75	Mike McCormack	16– 25– 1
1976–82	Dick Vermeil	57– 51– 0
1983–85	Marion Campbell	17– 29– 1
1985	Fred Bruney	1– 0– 0
1986–90	Buddy Ryan	43– 38– 1

Titles: 1947 (NFL East), 1948 (NFL), 1949 (NFL), 1960 (NFL), 1980 (NFC), 1988 (NFC East).

History: The Eagles were founded by Bert Bell and Lud Wray in 1933 after the state of Pennsylvania repealed a law banning sports on Sundays. In the late 1940s, the Eagles were one of the best teams in NFL history, playing in three consecutive title games and winning in 1948 and 1949, both by shutouts. In 1960 The Eagles returned to the top, when quarterback Norm Van Brocklin, by the sheer force of his personality, took a bunch of average players to the NFL title. From 1978 to 1981 head coach Dick Vermeil made the Eagles one of the top teams in the NFL, taking them all the way to Super Bowl XV following the 1980 season. These teams were led by quarterback Ron Jaworski and wide receiver Harold Carmichael, who set an NFL record (since broken) by catching a pass in 127 consecutive games.

Did You Know?: Former Eagles head coach Joe Kuharich made what is frequently considered the worst trade of all time in 1964. That year he sent quarterback Sonny Jurgensen – arguably the best passer in the history of pro football – to the Washington Redskins for quarterback Norm Snead, a solid player, but one hardly in the category of Jurgensen.

PHOENIX CARDINALS

Address: P.O. Box 888, Phoenix, Arizona 85001–0888.
Telephone: (602) 967–1010.
Stadium: Sun Devil Stadium.
Stadium Facts: capacity: 72,000; playing surface: Grass.
Record Attendance: 67,139 vs. Dallas, 12 September 1988.
Record Margin of Victory: 60 (60–0) vs. Rochester, 7 October 1923.
Record Margin of Loss: 46 (53–7) vs. Chicago Bears, 12 October 1941.
Team Colours: Cardinal Red, Black, and White.
President: William V. Bidwill.
Head Coach: Joe Bugel.
Some Notable Cardinals: Ottis Anderson, Jim Bakken, Dan Dierdorf, Pat Harder, Jim Hart, Mal Kutner, Jackie Smith, Roger Wehrli.

Cardinals Coaching History:

1920–22	John (Paddy) Driscoll	17–	8–	4
1923–24	Arnold Horween	13–	8–	1
1925–26	Norm Barry	16–	8–	2
1927	Guy Chamberlin	3–	7–	1
1928	Fred Gillies	1–	5–	0
1929	Dewey Scanlon	6–	6–	1
1930	Ernie Nevers	5–	3–	0
1931	LeRoy Andrews	0–	1–	0
1931	Ernie Nevers	5–	3–	0
1932	Jack Chevigny	2–	6–	2
1933–34	Paul Schissler	6–	15–	1
1935–38	Milan Creighton	16–	26–	4
1939	Ernie Nevers	1–	10–	0

1940–42	Jimmy Conzelman	8–	22–	3
1943–45	Phil Handler	1–	29–	0
1946–48	Jimmy Conzelman	27–	10–	0
1949	Phil Handler–Buddy Parker	2–	4–	0
1949	Raymond (Buddy) Parker	4–	1–	1
1950–51	Earl (Curly) Lambeau	7–	15–	0
1951	Phil Handler–Cecil Isbell	1–	1–	0
1952	Joe Kuharich	4–	8–	0
1953–54	Joe Stydahar	3–	20–	1
1955–57	Ray Richards	14–	21–	1
1958–61	Frank (Pop) Ivy	17–	29–	2
1961	Chuck Drulis–Ray Prochaska–Ray Willsey	2–	0–	0
1962–65	Walley Lemm	27–	26–	3
1966–70	Charley Winner	35–	30–	5
1971–72	Bob Hollway	8–	18–	2
1973–77	Don Coryell	42–	29–	1
1978–79	Bud Wilkinson	9–	20–	0
1979	Larry Wilson	2–	1–	0
1980–85	Jim Hanifan	39–	50–	1
1986–89	Gene Stallings	23–	34–	1
1989	Hank Kuhlmann	0–	5–	0
1990	Joe Bugel	5–	11–	0

Titles: 1925 (NFL), 1947 (NFL), 1948 (NFL West), 1974 (NFC East), 1975 (NFC East).

History: The oldest team in the NFL, first organized in Chicago in 1899 by Chris O'Brien under the name of the Morgan Athletic Club. The team name was later changed to the Normals and then to the Cardinals. O'Brien's team entered the NFL in 1920 as the Racine Cardinals, named for a street in south Chicago. In 1929 O'Brien sold the Cardinals to Dr. David Jones, who, in turn, sold them in 1933 to Charles W. Bidwill, the father of the current owner. The Cardinals' last title came in 1947, when they beat Philadelphia 28-21 in the title game.

> *Did You Know?*: The Cardinals have had three long-term homes. From 1899 to 1959 they played in Chicago. From 1960 to 1987 they represented St. Louis. And since 1988 they have been located in Phoenix.

PITTSBURGH STEELERS

Address: Three Rivers Stadium, 300 Stadium Circle, Pittsburgh, Pennsylvania 15212.
Telephone: (412) 323-1200.
Stadium: Three Rivers Stadium.
Stadium Facts: capacity: 59,000; playing surface: AstroTurf.
Record Attendance: 59,541 vs. Cincinnati, 30 September 1985.
Record Margin of Victory: 56 (63–7) vs. N.Y. Giants, 30 November 1952.
Record Margin of Loss: 47 (47–0) vs. Green Bay, 15 October 1933; (54–7) vs. Green Bay, 23 November 1941.
Team Colors: Black and Gold.
President: Daniel M. Rooney.
Head Coach: Chuck Noll.
Some Notable Steelers: Buddy Dial, L. C. Greenwood, Dick Hoak, Andy Russell, Donnie Shell, John Stallworth, Lynn Swann, Mike Webster.

Steelers Coaching History:

1933	Forrest (Jap) Douds	3–	6– 2
1934	Luby DiMelio	2–	10– 0
1935–36	Joe Bach	10–	14– 0
1937–39	Johnny Blood (McNally)	6–	19– 0
1939–40	Walt Kiesling	3–	13– 3
1941	Bert Bell	0–	2– 0
1941	Aldo (Buff) Donelli	0–	5– 0
1941–44	Walt Kiesling	13–	20– 2
1945	Jim Leonard	2–	8– 0
1946–47	Jock Sutherland	13–	10– 1

1948–51	Johnny Michelosen	20– 26– 2
1952–53	Joe Bach	11– 13– 0
1954–56	Walt Kiesling	14– 22– 0
1957–64	Raymond (Buddy) Parker	51– 47– 6
1965	Mike Nixon	2– 12– 0
1966–68	Bill Austin	11– 28– 3
1969–90	Chuck Noll	202–147– 1

Titles: 1972 (AFC Central), 1974 (Super Bowl IX), 1975 (Super Bowl X), 1976 (AFC Central), 1977 (AFC Central), 1978 (Super Bowl XIII), 1979 (Super Bowl XIV), 1983 (AFC Central), 1984 (AFC Central).

History: The Steelers were founded as the Pittsburgh Pirates in 1933 by Art Rooney, who purchased an NFL franchise with the winnings from a great day at the race track. In 1940 Rooney sold the Pirates to Alexis Thompson, but the next year he got his team back and renamed it the Steelers. The Steelers were persistent losers until Chuck Noll became head coach in 1969 and started drafting players such as defensive tackle Joe Greene, quarterback Terry Bradshaw, and running back Franco Harris. Three years later, Noll had his team in the playoffs, and two years after that they won Super Bowl IX. The Steelers won four Super Bowls in six years to earn praise as one of the greatest teams of all time. In recent years, after losing his star veterans, Noll has rebuilt the Steelers into a tough team of playoff caliber.

Did You Know?: In 1972 the Steelers earned their first playoff victory ever with one of the most bizarre game finishes in NFL history. With 22 seconds left, the Steelers trailed the Raiders 7-6 and faced a fourth-and-10 at their own 40. Bradshaw threw a pass to running back Frenchy Fuqua, but it was deflected by Oakland safety Jack Tatum. Harris caught the ball at his shoe tops in full stride and carried it in for the winning touchdown, on a play since named 'The Immaculate Reception'.

SAN DIEGO CHARGERS

Address: San Diego Jack Murphy Stadium, P.O. Box 20666, San Diego, California 92120.
Telephone: (619) 280-2111.
Stadium: San Diego Jack Murphy Stadium.
Stadium Facts: capacity: 60,750; playing surface: Grass.
Record Attendance: 61,660 vs. Denver, 29 November 1987.
Record Margin of Victory: 46 (53-7) vs. N.Y. Jets, 2 November 1963.
Record Margin of Loss: 43 (49-6) vs. Kansas City, 13 December 1964.
Team Colors: Navy Blue, White, and Gold.
Chairman of the Board/President: Alex G. Spanos.
Head Coach: Dan Henning.
Some Notable Chargers: Dan Fouts, Gary Garrison, John Hadl, Charlie Joiner, Dickie Post, Walt Sweeney, Russ Washington, Kellen Winslow.

Chargers Coaching History:

1960–69	Sid Gillman	83–	51– 6
1969–70	Charlie Waller	9–	7– 3
1971	Sid Gillman	4–	6– 0
1971–73	Harland Svare	7–	17– 2
1973	Ron Waller	1–	5– 0
1974–78	Tommy Prothro	21–	39– 0
1978–86	Don Coryell	72–	60– 0
1986–88	Al Saunders	17–	22– 0
1989–90	Dan Henning	12–	20– 0

Titles: 1960 (AFL West), 1961 (AFL West), 1963 (AFL),

1964 (AFL West), 1965 (AFL West), 1979 (AFC West),
1980 (AFC West), 1981 (AFC West).

History: The Chargers were founded as one of the original
six AFL teams. They were located in Los Angeles their first
year, but then moved to San Diego. The Chargers have
always been known for their devastating offenses. In the
early 1960s, when they played in five AFL title games in six
years, offensive genius Sid Gillman's team was led by
quarterback Jack Kemp, flanker Lance Alworth, and
running backs Paul Lowe and Keith Lincoln. In the late
1960s, the stars were quarterback John Hadl, receivers
Alworth and Gary Garrison, and running back Dickie
Post. A decade later, Don Coryell continued Gillman's
passing tradition with quarterback Dan Fouts, wide
receivers John Jefferson, Charlie Joiner and Wes
Chandler, and tight end Kellen Winslow. This group led
the Chargers to four consecutive playoff appearances,
1979–82.

Did You Know: The Chargers received their team name
because their original owner – Barron Hilton – liked its
three different implications – an electrical charge (later
indicated by lightning bolts on the Chargers' helmets), a
horse charging (which was the symbol on the club's
stationery), and the new Hilton Carte Blanche charge
card.

SAN FRANCISCO 49ERS

Address: 4949 Centennial Boulevard, Santa Clara,
California 95054.
Telephone: (408) 562-4949.
Stadium: Candlestick Park.
Stadium Facts: capacity: 65,729; playing surface: Grass.
Record Attendance: 64,250 vs. L.A. Rams, 1 October
1989.
Record Margin of Victory: 49 (49-0) vs. Detroit, 1 October
1961.
Record Margin of Loss: 49 (56-7) vs. L.A. Rams, 9
November 1958.
Team Colors: Forty Niners Gold and Scarlet.
Owner/President: Edward J. DeBartolo, Jr.
Head Coach: George Seifert.
Some Notable 49ers: John Brodie, Charlie Krueger,
Jimmy Johnson, Ronnie Lott, Joe Montana, Jerry Rice,
Dave Wilcox, Ken Willard.

49ers Coaching History:

1946–54	Lawrence (Buck) Shaw	72–	40–	4
1955	Norman (Red) Strader	4–	8–	0
1956–58	Frankie Albert	19–	17–	1
1959–63	Howard (Red) Hickey	27–	27–	1
1963–67	Jack Christiansen	26–	38–	3
1968–75	Dick Nolan	56–	56–	5
1976	Monte Clark	8–	6–	0
1977	Ken Meyer	5–	9–	0
1978	Pete McCulley	1–	8–	0
1978	Fred O'Connor	1–	6–	0
1979–88	Bill Walsh	102–	63–	1

1989–90 George Seifert 32– 5– 0

Titles: 1970 (NFC West), 1971 (NFC West), 1972 (NFC West), 1981 (Super Bowl XVI), 1983 (NFC West), 1984 (Super Bowl XIX), 1986 (NFC West), 1987 (NFC West), 1988 (Super Bowl XXIII), 1989 (Super Bowl XXIV), 1990 (NFC West).

History: The 49ers were one of the original All-America Football Conference teams in 1946, and joined the NFL in 1950 following the death of the AAFC. In the mid-1950s, the 49ers had one of the greatest offensive backfields of all time, with all four players destined for the Hall of Fame: quarterback Y.A. Tittle, fullback Joe Perry, and halfbacks Hugh (The King) McElhenny and John Henry Johnson. Despite a long list of great players, the 49ers never won even a division title until 1970, when they won the NFC West for the first of three consecutive years. The 49ers' greatest success came in the 1980s, however, when four times they achieved the best regular-season record, and when they also won four Super Bowl titles.

Did You Know?: The most satisfying game in 49ers history is not usually considered to be any of their Super Bowl victories, but their 28–27 victory over the Dallas Cowboys in the 1981 NFC Championship Game that put them in their first Super Bowl. The 49ers climaxed an 89-yard drive with 51 seconds left in the game, when Joe Montana threw a six-yard touchdown pass to wide receiver Dwight Clark.

SEATTLE SEAHAWKS

Address: 11220 N.E. 53rd Street, Kirkland, Washington 98033.
Telephone: (206) 827-9777.
Stadium: Kingdome.
Stadium Facts: capacity: 64,984; playing surface: AstroTurf.
Record Attendance: 64,411 vs. Denver, 15 December 1984.
Record Margin of Victory: 45 (45–0) vs. Kansas City, 4 November 1984.
Record Margin of Loss: 44 (51–7) vs. Dallas, 27 November 1980.
Team Colors: Blue, Green, and Silver.
Owner: Ken Behring.
Head Coach: Chuck Knox.
Some Notable Seahawks: Dave Brown, Kenny Easley, Jacob Green, Dave Krieg, Steve Largent, Curt Warner, Fredd Young, Jim Zorn.

Seahawks Coaching History:

1976–82	Jack Patera		35– 59– 0
1982	Mike McCormack		4– 3– 0
1983–90	Chuck Knox		76– 58– 0

Titles: 1988 (AFC West).

History: Seattle was one of two expansion franchises (along with Tampa Bay) in 1976. The Seahawks were in the NFC West their first year, before being transferred to the AFC West. Seattle achieved a winning record (9–7) in only its third year in the NFL, but the Seahawks did not make the playoffs until 1983, when they hired Chuck Knox as head coach. In his first year, Knox guided his team to the AFC Championship Game, and the next year the Seahawks recorded their best record ever, 12–4. The Seahawks originally were primarily a passing team, moving on the arm of quarterback Jim Zorn, but Knox built a powerful ground attack spearheaded by running backs Curt Warner and John L. Williams and supplemented by the passing of Dave Krieg.

Did You Know: In 1976 the Seahawks obtained rookie wide receiver Steve Largent from Houston for a sixth-round draft choice. Largent went on to lead the Seahawks in receiving 12 consecutive years, to register eight 1,000-yard seasons, and to become the NFL's career leader in receptions (819), receiving yards (13,089), and touchdown receptions (100).

TAMPA BAY BUCCANEERS

Address: One Buccaneer Place, Tampa, Florida 33607.
Telephone: (813) 870-2700.
Stadium: Tampa Stadium.
Stadium Facts: capacity: 74,315; playing surface: Grass.
Record Attendance: 72,077 vs. Chicago, 8 October 1989.
Record Margin of Victory: 38 (48–10) vs. Atlanta, 13
September 1987.
Record Margin of Loss: 42 (42–0) vs. Pittsburgh, 5
December 1976.
Team Colors: Florida Orange, White, and Red.
Owner-President: Hugh F. Culverhouse.
Head Coach: Richard Williamson.
Some Notable Buccaneers: Ricky Bell, Jimmie Giles,
Hugh Green, Kevin House, Lee Roy Selmon, Vinny
Testaverde, James Wilder, Doug Williams.

Buccaneers Coaching History:

1976-84	John McKay		45- 91- 1
1985-86	Leeman Bennett		4- 28- 0
1987-90	Ray Perkins		19- 41- 0
1990	Richard Williamson		1- 2- 0

Titles: 1979 (NFC Central), 1981 (NFC Central).

History: Tampa Bay joined the NFL as an expansion team
in 1976. The Buccaneers were originally the fifth team in
the AFC West, but moved the next year to the NFC
Central. The Buccaneers became the first 0-14 team in
NFL history their first season, losing to each of the other
AFC teams and to Seattle (13-10). Their losing streak
increased to 26 before they finally defeated New Orleans
33-14 in 1977. Remarkably, two years later Tampa Bay

won the NFC Central title and proceeded to the NFC Championship Game, where the Los Angeles Rams won 9–0. That 1979 team and its successors had one of the best defenses in the NFL, led by superstar defensive end Lee Roy Selmon and linebackers Hugh Green and David Lewis. The Buccaneers' offense was powered first by the running of Ricky Bell and then by the running and receiving of James Wilder.

> *Did You Know?*: The Buccaneers have had the number-one selection in the draft four times. Their choices have been Lee Roy Selmon, who should soon be selected to the Hall of Fame; Ricky Bell, a super running back until his untimely death; Bo Jackson, who has gone on to fame in baseball and with the Los Angeles Raiders; and Vinny Testaverde, a former Heisman Trophy winner who is Tampa Bay's current quarterback.

WASHINGTON REDSKINS

Address: Redskin Park, P.O. Box 17247, Dulles
International Airport, Washington, D.C. 20041.
Telephone: (703) 471-9100.
Stadium: Robert F. Kennedy Stadium.
Stadium Facts: capacity: 55,672; playing surface: Grass.
Record Attendance: 55,750 vs. Dallas, 10 November 1985.
Record Margin of Victory: 44 (51-7) vs. L.A. Rams, 1
January 1984 (NFC Divisional Playoff Game).
Record Margin of Loss: 73 (73-0) vs. Chicago Bears, 8
December 1940 (NFL Championship Game).
Team Colors: Burgundy and Gold.
Chairman of the Board-CEO: Jack Kent Cooke.
Head Coach: Joe Gibbs.
Some Notable Redskins: Gene Brito, Larry Brown, Chris
Hanburger, Billy Kilmer, Art Monk, John Riggins, Jerry
Smith, Joe Theismann.

Redskins Coaching History:

1932	Lud Wray	4-	4-	2
1933-34	William (Lone Star) Dietz	11-	11-	2
1935	Eddie Casey	2-	8-	1
1936-42	Ray Flaherty	56-	23-	3
1943	Arthur (Dutch) Bergman	7-	4-	1
1944-45	Dudley DeGroot	14-	6-	1
1946-48	Glen (Turk) Edwards	16-	18-	1
1949	John Whelchel	3-	3-	1
1949-51	Herman Ball	4-	16-	0
1951	Dick Todd	5-	4-	0
1952-53	Earl (Curly) Lambeau	10-	13-	1
1954-58	Joe Kuharich	26-	32-	2

1959–60	Mike Nixon	4– 18– 2
1961–65	Bill McPeak	21– 46– 3
1966–68	Otto Graham	17– 22– 3
1969	Vince Lombardi	7– 5– 2
1970	Bill Austin	6– 8– 0
1971–77	George Allen	69– 35– 1
1978–80	Jack Pardee	24– 24– 0
1981–90	Joe Gibbs	113– 55– 0

Titles: 1936 (NFL East), 1937 (NFL), 1940 (NFL East), 1942 (NFL), 1943 (NFL East), 1945 (NFL East), 1972 (NFC), 1982 (Super Bowl XVII), 1983 (NFC), 1984 (NFC East), 1987 (Super Bowl XXII).

History: The Redskins were founded in 1932 as the Boston Braves, but the next year their name was changed to the Redskins. In 1937 their owner, George Preston Marshall, disappointed by small attendance – even though the Redskins had won the NFL East the previous year – moved his club to Washington. The Redskins were one of the top teams between 1936 and 1945, playing in the NFL title game six times in that decade. However, they did not return to prominence until George Allen became coach in 1971 and led them to the playoffs five times in six years. Washington's third great era was the 1980s. Under Joe Gibbs, the Redskins made the playoffs five times in six years, winning the NFC title three times and the Super Bowl championship twice.

Did You Know?: Sammy Baugh, the Redskins' great quarterback of the 1930s and 1940s is sometimes considered the best all-purpose player ever. In 1943, he led the NFL in passing, in punting, and in interceptions (with 11, the most-ever at the time). He not only led the league's passers a record six times, he led in punting four times and is the career punting leader.

SUPER BOWL RESULTS

Game	Date	Winner		Loser		Attendance
I	15-1-67	Green Bay	35	Kansas City	10	61,946
II	14-1-68	Green Bay	33	Oakland	14	75,546
III	12-1-69	N.Y. Jets	16	Baltimore	7	75,389
IV	11-1-70	Kansas City	23	Minnesota	7	80,562
V	17-1-71	Baltimore	16	Dallas	13	79,204
VI	16-1-72	Dallas	24	Miami	3	81,023
VII	14-1-73	Miami	14	Washington	7	90,182
VIII	13-1-74	Miami	24	Minnesota	7	71,882
IX	12-1-75	Pittsburgh	16	Minnesota	6	80,997
X	18-1-76	Pittsburgh	21	Dallas	17	80,187
XI	9-1-77	Oakland	32	Minnesota	14	103,438
XII	15-1-78	Dallas	27	Denver	10	75,583
XIII	21-1-79	Pittsburgh	35	Dallas	31	79,484
XIV	20-1-80	Pittsburgh	31	L.A. Rams	19	103,985
XV	25-1-81	Oakland	27	Philadelphia	10	76,135
XVI	24-1-82	San Francisco	26	Cincinnati	21	81,270
XVII	30-1-83	Washington	27	Miami	17	103,667
XVIII	22-1-84	L.A. Raiders	38	Washington	9	72,920
XIX	20-1-85	San Francisco	38	Miami	16	84,059
XX	26-1-86	Chicago	46	New England	10	73,818
XXI	25-1-87	N.Y. Giants	39	Denver	20	101,063
XXII	31-1-88	Washington	42	Denver	10	73,302
XXIII	22-1-89	San Francisco	20	Cincinnati	16	75,129
XXIV	28-1-90	San Francisco	55	Denver	10	72,919
XXV	27-1-91	N.Y. Giants	20	Buffalo	19	73,813

SUPER BOWL I

Green Bay 35, Kansas City 10
Los Angeles Memorial Coliseum
15 January 1967

Bart Starr, Tony Tomsic/NFL Photos.

The Green Bay Packers, the champions of the NFL, broke open a game that was close at halftime and defeated the AFL champion Kansas City Chiefs 35–10 in the first Super Bowl, officially designated the AFL–NFL World Championship Game.

The Packers opened the scoring midway through the first quarter, when Packers quarterback Bart Starr froze the Chiefs' secondary with a play-action fake and then passed to split end Max McGee. The ball was thrown behind McGee, who caught it with one hand, balanced the ball on his hip, and outran the Chiefs the remaining 19 yards to complete the 37-yard touchdown play. The 34-year-old McGee was only playing because starter Boyd Dowler had been injured on the second play of the game.

Kansas City tied the score 7–7 in the second quarter when quarterback Len Dawson finished a 66-yard drive with a seven-yard touchdown pass to fullback Curtis McClinton. The Packers scored on their next possession, driving 73 yards in 14 plays, with fullback Jim Taylor sweeping left from 14 yards out. The Chiefs kicked a field goal to make the margin 14–10 at the half.

On the opening drive of the second half, defensive tackle Henry Jordan hit Dawson's arm as he was attempting to pass. The ball was intercepted by safety Willie Wood and returned 50 yards to the Kansas City 5. On the next play, halfback Elijah Pitts went behind left tackle to score and break the back of the Chiefs. Kansas City did not threaten again, and Green Bay scored twice more, once on another pass from Starr, who was selected the game's most valuable player, to McGee.

SUPER BOWL II

Green Bay 33, Oakland 14
Orange Bowl, Miami
14 January 1968

Vince Lombardi, Tony Tomsic/NFL Photos.

The Green Bay Packers methodically picked apart the talented, but young, Oakland Raiders to win their second consecutive Super Bowl, 33–14. The Packers slowly built their lead, with Don Chandler kicking a field after each of their first two possessions. Then Green Bay struck quickly. On first down, after the Raiders had punted, split end Boyd Dowler raced by cornerback Kent McCloughan and caught a pass in full stride, for a 62-yard touchdown play.

On the following series, the Raiders drove 78 yards in nine plays for their first score. Quarterback Daryle Lamonica completed four of five passes, the last a 23-yard touchdown to split end Bill Miller. But the Packers extended their lead to 16–7 when Chandler kicked his third field goal on the last play of the half.

The Packers broke the game open in the third quarter, just as they had in Super Bowl I. On their second possession, they drove 82 yards in 11 plays, with halfback Donny Anderson smashing over from two yards out. Another field goal increased their lead to 26–7. Early in the fourth quarter, cornerback Herb Adderley intercepted a pass by Lamonica and raced 60 yards down the sidelines for Green Bay's final touchdown. Lamonica later passed to Miller for another score to make the final score less humiliating. For the second year in a row, Starr, who completed 13 of 24 passes for 202 yards, was named the game's most valuable player.

SUPER BOWL III

New York Jets 16, Baltimore 7
Orange Bowl, Miami
12 January 1969

Matt Snell, Vernon Biever/NFL Photos.

The New York Jets shocked the Baltimore Colts 16–7 to become the first AFL team to win the Super Bowl. Although the Colts were considered one of the greatest teams in the history of pro football, and were favored to win by three touchdowns, the Jets' brash quarterback, Joe Namath, guaranteed a victory three nights before the game. His team then followed through.

The Jets set the tone early in the game. On the second play from scrimmage, fullback Matt Snell gained nine yards before being tackled by all-pro safety Rick Volk, one of the toughest players in all of football. But Volk was knocked unconscious on the play and had to leave the game. The Jets had learned the Colts were human, and they knew they could compete.

In the second quarter, the Jets took the lead when Snell ended a 12-play, 80-yard drive with a four-yard touchdown run off left tackle. Snell would go on to set a Super Bowl record with 121 yards on 30 carries. Meanwhile, the Colts self-destructed, with NFL player of the year Earl Morrall throwing three interceptions and several times missing receivers who were open for easy touchdowns. Even the play of halfback Tom Matte, who gained 116 yards on only 11 carries, could not keep the Colts functioning effectively.

In the second half, the Jets chipped away, as Jim Turner kicked three field goals to increase their lead to 16-0. Late in the game, Morrall was replaced by Johnny Unitas – who had missed most of the season with injuries – and he led the Colts to a consolation touchdown. Namath, who completed 17 of 28 passes for 206 yards, was named the game's most valuable player over Snell.

SUPER BOWL IV

Kansas City 23, Minnesota 7
Tulane Stadium, New Orleans
11 January 1970

Len Dawson, Tony Tomsic
/NFL Photos.

The AFL squared the Super Bowl at two games apiece in
the final contest before the two leagues merged into one.
The game's most valuable player was Kansas City
quarterback Len Dawson, who completed 12 of 17 passes
for 142 yards and called a virtually flawless game despite
having missed six games during the regular season with a
knee injury.

The Chiefs were two-touchdown underdogs, but they
never trailed. On first possession, they marched 42 yards to
set up Jan Stenerud's 48-yard field goal, the longest in
Super Bowl history at the time. They moved 55 yards to
Stenerud's 32-yard field goal on their second possession,
and then they went 27 yards to set up his 25-yarder the
third time they got the ball. Minnesota's Charlie West
fumbled the kickoff after Stenerud's third field goal, and
Remi Prudhomme recovered for Kansas City at the
Minnesota 19. Six plays later, from the 5-yard-line, the
Chiefs' line pulled one way, the Vikings gave pursuit, and
halfback Mike Garrett cut against the grain and scored for
a 16–0 halftime lead.

Meanwhile, the Kansas City defense stifled the Vikings,
who gained only 67 yards rushing during the game and
were intercepted three times. Minnesota did have one
successful drive in the third quarter, moving 69 yards in 10
plays, culminating in a four-yard touchdown run by
running back Dave Osborn.

But Kansas City immediately responded with a
knockout punch. Starting from their own 18, the Chiefs
drove to the Minnesota 46. Then Dawson threw a short
pass to flanker Otis Taylor, who caught the ball in front of
cornerback Earsell Mackbee. Taylor simply ran through
Mackbee, faked out safety Karl Kassulke, and scored to
give the game its final margin.

SUPER BOWL V

Baltimore 16, Dallas 13
Orange Bowl, Miami
17 January 1971

Chuck Howley, NFL Photos.

Jim O'Brien's 32-yard field goal with five seconds remaining in the game gave Baltimore a 16–13 victory over the Dallas Cowboys in a game marked by 11 turnovers and 14 penalties, and since nicknamed the 'Blunder Bowl'.

Dallas opened the scoring when Mike Clark kicked a 14-yard field goal after safety Cliff Harris recovered Ron Gardin's fumble on a punt return at the Baltimore 9. Early in the second quarter, Clark's 30-yard field goal increased the margin to 6–0.

Baltimore tied the game 42 seconds later. On the third play after the kickoff, quarterback Johnny Unitas threw a medium-deep pass to Eddie Hinton. Hinton tipped the ball, as did cornerback Mel Renfro. Colts tight end John Mackey, who was running free behind the defense, caught the tip at the Dallas 45 and ran untouched to the end zone, completing a 75-yard scoring play. O'Brien's point after touchdown was blocked by Mark Washington.

Dallas moved back in front after Unitas fumbled and defensive tackle Jethro Pugh recovered at the Baltimore 28. Three plays later, quarterback Craig Morton threw a seven-yard touchdown pass to rookie running back Duane Thomas. The Cowboys had a chance to extend their lead in the third quarter, but Thomas fumbled on the Baltimore 1, and cornerback Jim Duncan recovered for the Colts.

Midway through the fourth quarter, Baltimore safety Rick Volk intercepted a pass from Morton and returned it 30 yards to the Dallas 3. Fullback Tom Nowatzke scored on the second play to tie the game 13–13. With 1:09 remaining, Baltimore linebacker Mike Curtis intercepted another of Morton's passes and returned it to the Dallas 28 to set up the winning field goal. The game's most valuable player was Dallas linebacker Chuck Howley, who made two interceptions and a multitude of tackles to become the only player from a losing team ever to be so honored.

SUPER BOWL VI

Dallas 24, Miami 3
Tulane Stadium, New Orleans
16 January 1972

Walt Garrison, Vernon Biever/NFL Photos.

The Dallas Cowboys, whom many experts felt had been the best team in football over the previous five years, finally won their first Super Bowl title by playing nearly a flawless game in routing the Miami Dolphins 24–3. It was a complete offensive and defensive effort, as the Cowboys set a Super Bowl record with 252 yards rushing, holding Miami to the lowest point total in a Super Bowl.

Dallas took an early lead when Mike Clark kicked a nine-yard field goal following linebacker Chuck Howley's recovery of Larry Csonka's fumble on the Dallas 48. The Dallas defense was evident again on the next series. On third and nine at the Miami 38, quarterback Bob Griese dropped back to pass; with no receivers open, he scrambled, trying to avoid defensive tackle Bob Lilly, who finally ran him down for a 29-yard loss.

Dallas moved ahead 10–0 with a 10-play, 76-yard drive that ended with a seven-yard touchdown pass from Roger Staubach to wide receiver Lance Alworth. The Dolphins cut the score to 10–3 with a field goal four seconds before the half, but the Cowboys wasted no time opening up the game in the third quarter. They took the second-half kickoff and went 71 yards in eight plays, with Duane Thomas scoring from the 3. Early in the fourth quarter, Howley intercepted a pass by Griese and returned it 41 yards to the Miami 9. Three plays later, Staubach passed seven yards to tight end Mike Ditka for a touchdown.

Staubach, who completed 12 of 19 passes for 119 yards, was named the game's most valuable player over Thomas, who gained 95 yards rushing on 19 carries, and Walt Garrison, who had 74 yards on 14 carries.

SUPER BOWL VII

Miami 14, Washington 7
Los Angeles Memorial Coliseum
14 January 1973

Jake Scott-interception, NFL Photos.

The Miami Dolphins defeated the Washington Redskins 14–7 to complete a season in which they won all 17 of their games, to become the first perfect-record team in NFL history. The Dolphins, who were actually two-point underdogs, shut down NFL rushing leader Larry Brown and were never seriously threatened.

The Dolphins took a 7–0 lead on their third possession, moving 63 yards in six plays and scoring on a 28-yard pass from quarterback Bob Griese to wide receiver Howard Twilley, who ran inside then outside on his pattern, turning cornerback Pat Fischer completely around.

The Dolphins increased their lead to 14–0 18 seconds before halftime. Following an interception by middle linebacker Nick Buoniconti, running back Jim Kiick scored from the 1 behind the blocking of Larry Little.

Both teams missed opportunities to score in the second half. Redskins safety Brig Owens intercepted Griese in the Washington end zone in the third quarter, and Miami safety Jake Scott returned the favor in the fourth quarter. The Redskins had driven 79 yards before Scott – named mvp – picked off quarterback Billy Kilmer's pass and returned it 55 yards to the Washington 48.

Strangely, Scott's interception was the prelude to the Redskins' only score. When Miami tried a field goal several plays later, the snap was high, and Garo Yepremian's kick was blocked. Yepremian picked up the ball and attempted to pass, but it slipped out of his hands and was plucked out of the air by cornerback Mike Bass, who ran 49 yards for a Washington touchdown, the final score of the day.

SUPER BOWL VIII

**Miami 24, Minnesota 7
Rice Stadium, Houston
13 January 1974**

*Larry Czonka, Malcolm Emmons
/NFL Photos.*

Miami completely controlled the Minnesota Vikings from the very start of the game to earn an easy 24–7 victory in a contest in which the Dolphins became the first (and still the only) team to appear in three consecutive Super Bowls.

Following the opening kickoff, Miami moved 62 yards in 10 plays, scoring on fullback Larry Csonka's five-yard run. After Minnesota ran three plays and punted, Miami marched 56 yards in 10 plays, scoring on Jim Kiick's one-yard run. At the end of the first quarter, Miami not only led 14–0, the Dolphins had gained 118 yards and eight first downs on 20 plays. Minnesota had run just six plays for 25 yards and one first down.

In the second quarter, the Dolphins increased their lead to 17–0, going 44 yards in seven plays for Garo Yepremian's 28-yard field goal. Minnesota's only effective drive ended when running back Oscar Reed fumbled and Miami safety Jake Scott recovered at the Miami 6.

The Dolphins put the game totally out of reach in the third quarter. With the ball on the Minnesota 2, quarterback Bob Griese forgot the number of which the ball was supposed to be snapped. He asked Csonka what the number was, and the fullback said two, but Kiick said it was one. Griese finally agreed with Csonka, but then center Jim Langer snapped the ball on one. Griese juggled it, and barely handed off to Csonka, who followed guard Larry Little and tackle Norm Evans into the end zone. For the day, Csonka gained a Super Bowl record 145 yards on 33 carries; he was named the game's most valuable player.

SUPER BOWL IX

Pittsburgh 16, Minnesota 6
Tulane Stadium, New Orleans
12 January 1975

Franco Harris, NFL Photos.

Pittsburgh fullback Franco Harris set Super Bowl records by rushing 34 times for 158 yards, while the Steelers' defense held the Minnesota Vikings to only 17 yards on the ground in a 16–6 Pittsburgh victory, which gave the club its first league championship in its 42-year history.

The Steelers led only 2–0 at halftime after each team squandered several scoring opportunities. The only score came midway through the second quarter, when Minnesota quarterbacck Frank Tarkenton fumbled when trying to hand off to running back Dave Osborn. Attempting to regain possession of the ball, Tarkenton slid into the end zone, where he was downed by defensive end Dwight White for a safety.

Bill Brown of Minnesota fumbled the second-half kickoff, and Pittsburgh's Marv Kellum recovered at the Vikings' 30. Four plays later, Harris, who was named the game's most valuable player, scored on a nine-yard run to make it 9–0.

Early in the fourth quarter, Minnesota linebacker Matt Blair blocked Bobby Walden's punt at the 15-yard line, and the ball was recovered in the end zone for a touchdown by the Vikings' Terry Brown. Fred Cox's extra point attempt missed.

The Steelers came right back with the game's final score. The two big plays of the drive were passes from quarterback Terry Bradshaw to tight end Larry Brown. The first was for 30 yards on third down – keeping the drive alive – and the second was a four-yard touchdown strike, again on third down.

For the game, the Steelers outgained the Vikings 333 yards to 119 and intercepted Tarkenton three times.

SUPER BOWL X

Pittsburgh 21, Dallas 17
Orange Bowl, Miami
18 January 1976

Lynn Swann, Heinz Kluetmeier/SE/NFL Photos.

In a game generally acclaimed the most exciting Super
Bowl to that point, the Pittsburgh Steelers edged the
Dallas Cowboys 21–17. After Pittsburgh's first possession,
punter Bobby Walden bobbled the snap from center and
was tackled at his 29 by Billy Joe DuPree. On the next
play, quarterback Roger Staubach threw a touchdown
pass to wide receiver Drew Pearson.

The Steelers answered, moving 67 yards in eight plays
and scoring on a seven-yard pass from Terry Bradshaw to
tight end Randy Grossman. Dallas moved ahead on the
next series with Toni Fritsch's 36-yard field goal.

Dallas maintained its 10–7 lead until early in the fourth
quarter. A safety, cut the Dallas lead to 10–9. Roy Gerela's
36-yard field goal gave the Steelers a 12–10 lead. On the
first play after the kickoff, safety Mike Wagner of the
Steelers intercepted a pass from Staubach, setting up
another field goal by Gerela, which made the score 15–10
with 6:37 left.

On Pittsburgh's next possession, Bradshaw passed 64
yards for a touchdown to Swann (mvp) for a 21–10 lead.

Dallas made a valiant comeback in the final three
minutes. Staubach first drove his team 80 yards in five
plays, throwing a 34-yard touchdown pass to wide receiver
Percy Howard. Then, taking possession on downs at their
own 39, Staubach passed them to the Pittsburgh 38. His
pass into the end zone was intercepted by safety Glen
Edwards on the last play of the game.

SUPER BOWL XI

Oakland 32, Minnesota 14
Rose Bowl, Pasadena
9 January 1977

Clarence Davis, Malcolm Emmons/NFL Photos.

The Oakland Raiders, the perpetual bridesmaid in the AFC (having lost in the conference championship game six times in the previous eight years), finally won a Super Bowl, and in so doing made the Minnesota Vikings the first four-time losers.

Late in the first quarter, Oakland's Ray Guy sustained the first blocked punt of his four-year NFL career, and Minnesota gained possession at the Oakland 3. But running back Brent McClanahan fumbled on second down, and linebacker Willie Hall recovered for Oakland. The Raiders then drove 90 yards in 12 plays to Errol Mann's 24-yard field goal.

The Raiders jumped to a big lead before halftime. First they drove 64 yards on 10 plays, scoring on quarterback Ken Stabler's one-yard pass to tight end Dave Casper. Then a 25-yard punt return by Neal Colzie set up Pete Banaszak's one-yard touchdown run, which gave Oakland a 16–0 halftime lead. After 30 minutes of play, the Raiders had outgained the Vikings 288 yards to 86 and 16 first downs to 4.

With the score 19–7 after three quarters, the Raiders iced the game on two defensive plays. First Hall intercepted one of Tarkenton's passes and returned it 16 yards; that set up a drive culminated by Banaszak's two-yard touchdown run. Then, on the Vikings' next possession, cornerback Willie Brown intercepted another pass and returned it 75 yards for a touchdown that made the score 32–7.

Fred Biletnikoff was named mvp.

SUPER BOWL XII

Dallas 27, Denver 10
Louisiana Superdome, New Orleans
15 January 1978

Harvey Martin sacks Norris Weese, PRM/NFL Photos.

The Dallas defense totally dominated the sputtering
Denver offense, intercepting four passes and recovering
three fumbles, in an easy 27–10 victory.

The difficulties for Denver quarterback Craig Morton in
moving against his former Dallas teammates began
immediately. Midway through the first quarter, safety
Randy Hughes intercepted one of Morton's passes, giving
Dallas the ball at the Denver 25. Five plays later, rookie
running back Tony Dorsett scored from three yards out.
On the next series, Morton was intercepted again, setting
up Efren Herrera's 35-yard field goal. The Cowboys
started the second quarter with another field goal.

Denver scored on Jim Turner's 47-yard field goal to start
the third quarter, but the Cowboys came right back with a
58-yard drive in only six plays. On third-and-10, Staubach
threw a 45-yard touchdown pass to Butch Johnson.

Denver responded with a touchdown of its own set up by
a 67-yard kickoff return by Rick Upchurch. After his first
pass was almost intercepted, Morton was replaced by
Norris Weese, and four plays later, running back Rob
Lytle scored to narrow the Dallas lead to 20–10. But once
again the Dallas defense took over. On Denver's next
possession, defensive end Harvey Martin recovered
Weese's fumble on the Denver 29. On the next play,
running back Robert Newhouse took a hand-off, went
wide left, stopped, and threw a pass to wide receiver
Golden Richards, who was alone in the end zone.

For the day, Dallas gained 325 yards, while holding
Denver to 156, including only 35 passing. Martin and
defensive tackle Randy White were named the game's co-
most valuable players.

SUPER BOWL XIII

Pittsburgh 35, Dallas 31
Orange Bowl, Miami
21 January 1979

Terry Bradshaw, John Biever/NFL Photos.

In the first Super Bowl rematch the Steelers became the first team to win three Super Bowls.

In the highest-scoring Super Bowl of all, Bradshaw (mvp) threw for a personal high 318 yards and broke Bart Starr's passing yardage record by halftime.

Bradshaw opened the scoring on Pittsburgh's first possession, throwing 28 yards to wide receiver John Stallworth. The Cowboys came back on the last play of the first quarter to tie it 7–7 when Roger Staubach passed to wide receiver Tony Hill for 39 yards and a score.

Dallas took its only lead of the game when linebacker Mike Hegman wrestled the ball away from Bradshaw early in the second quarter and ran 37 yards for a touchdown. Three plays later, the score was tied again, when Bradshaw threw a 75-yard touchdown pass to Stallworth. With 26 seconds remaining in the first half, Bradshaw completed a hurry-up drive with a seven-yard touchdown pass to running back Rocky Bleier.

Dallas cut the Pittsburgh lead to four points in the third quarter, but Rafael Septien's field goal was a moral victory for the Steelers. With third-and-three at the 10, Staubach passed to Jackie Smith, who dropped the pass.

In the fourth quarter, the Steelers scored twice within 19 seconds to go ahead 35–17. But the game was not over; Staubach got the Cowboys moving in one of his famous comebacks. Staubach capped an 89-yard drive with a seven-yard pass to tight end Billy Joe DuPree, and, after Dallas recovered an onside kick, threw another scoring pass to wide receiver Butch Johnson with 22 seconds left. But another onside kick attempt was recovered by Bleier to seal Pittsburgh's victory.

SUPER BOWL XIV

Pittsburgh 31, Los Angeles Rams 19
Rose Bowl, Pasadena
20 January 1980

Chuck Noll, Paul Spinelli/NFL Photos.

Quarterback Bradshaw (mvp) threw a 73-yard touchdown pass to wide receiver John Stallworth to bring the Steelers from behind early in the fourth quarter, and defeat the Los Angeles Rams 31–19 for their fourth Super Bowl victory in as many appearances.

After the Steelers took an early 3–0 lead, the Rams immediately drove 59 yards on eight plays for a one-yard scoring run by Cullen Bryant. The Steelers came right back, moving 53 yards in nine plays, with Franco Harris also scoring from a yard out. Again, the Rams responded immediately, driving 67 yards to a 31-yard field goal by Frank Corral that tied the game 10–10. Two series later, Dave Elmendorf intercepted one of Bradshaw's passes, and, with 12 seconds left in the half, Corral kicked a 45-yard field goal for a 13–10 Los Angeles lead.

The Steelers wasted little time in the second half getting back on top. A 37-yard kickoff return by Larry Anderson put them on their own 39, and five plays later Bradshaw threw a 47-yard touchdown pass to wide receiver Lynn Swann. But the Rams again matched them, this time in only four plays. A 50-yard pass from quarterback Vince Ferragamo to Billy Waddy put the Rams on the Pittsburgh 24. On the next play, Lawrence McCutcheon shocked the Steelers with a halfback pass to Ron Smith, good for a touchdown and a 19–17 lead.

That signalled the beginning of the Bradshaw-Stallworth air show that first put Pittsburgh ahead 24–19 and then set up Franco Harris' clinching one-yard run.

SUPER BOWL XV

Oakland 27, Philadelphia 10
Louisiana Superdome, New Orleans
25 January 1981

Rod Martin, MV Rubio/NFL Photos.

The Oakland defense, led by linebacker Rod Martin's three interceptions, set up 10 points and controlled the tempo of the game as the Raiders defeated Philadelphia 27–10. The win marked the first time that a wild-card team had won a Super Bowl.

Oakland took control early. On the third play of the game, Martin intercepted Philadelphia quarterback Ron Jaworksi's pass and returned it to the Eagles' 30. Seven plays later, Raiders quarterback Jim Plunkett threw the first of his three touchdown passes of the day, a two-yarder to wide receiver Cliff Branch.

Late in the first quarter, with a third-and-four from the Raiders' 20, Plunkett passed to running back Kenny King, who gathered the ball in at the Oakland 39 and raced down the left sideline 61 yards, completing an 80-yard touchdown, then the longest play in Super Bowl history.

Leading 14–3 at halftime, the Raiders applied the knockout punch early in the third quarter, driving 76 yards in only five plays. Plunkett passed to King for 13 yards, to wide receiver Bob Chandler for 32 yards, and then to Branch for 29 yards and a touchdown. When the Eagles tried to get back in the game on Jaworski's arm, Martin intercepted his second pass, setting up a 46-yard field goal by Chris Bahr, which increased the Raiders' lead to 24–3.

Jaworski led the Eagles to their only touchdown in the fourth quarter, an 88-yard drive capped by an eight-yard pass to tight end Keith Krepfle. But the day belonged to Martin, who intercepted Jaworski yet again in the waning moments of the game, and to Plunkett, who was named the game's most valuable player after completing 13 of 21 passes for 261 yards and three scores.

SUPER BOWL XVI

San Francisco 26, Cincinnati 21
Pontiac Silverdome
24 January 1982

49ers' defensive stand, Tony Tomsic/NFL Photos.

The San Francisco defense came up with big plays throughout the game, including a four-play goal-line stand late in the third quarter, to hold off Cincinnati's record-setting offense in a 26–21 victory.

The 49ers' defense set the tone early. After the Bengals recovered a fumble on the opening kickoff, safety Dwight Hicks intercepted Cincinnati quarterback Ken Anderson's pass at the 49ers' 5 and returned it to the 32. San Francisco then drove 68 yards, scoring on quarterback Joe Montana's one-yard run.

Early in the second quarter, the San Francisco defense thwarted another Cincinnati drive when cornerback Eric Wright stripped the ball loose from wide receiver Cris Collinsworth and the 49ers recovered at their 8. Twelve plays and 92 yards later, Montana threw an 11-yard touchdown pass to running back Earl Cooper. Two field goals late in the half gave the 49ers a 20–0 lead.

Cincinnati marched 83 yards to a touchdown to start the second half, Anderson scoring on a five-yard run. Late in the third quarter, the Bengals moved to a first-and-goal at the San Francisco 3. Fullback Pete Johnson gained two yards on first down, but the 49ers' defense rose to the occasion and stopped three successive plays from the 1.

A four-yard pass from Anderson to Dan Ross (who caught a Super Bowl record 11 passes) cut the margin to 20–14 in the fourth quarter, but the 49ers responded with two field goals for a 26–14 lead. Anderson led the Bengals 74 yards to a final touchdown with 16 seconds left, but an onside kick failed.

Montana, who had completed 14 of 22 passes for 157 yards, was named the game's most valuable player.

SUPER BOWL XVII

Washington 27, Miami 17
Rose Bowl, Pasadena
30 January 1983

John Riggins, Al Messerschmidt/NFL Photos.

Running back John Riggins pounded out 166 yards rushing, including the winning 43-yard touchdown run in the fourth quarter, and the Washington Redskins defeated the Miami Dolphins 27–17, to win their first NFL championship since 1942.

The Dolphins opened the scoring on their second possession, when quarterback David Woodley found wide receiver Jimmy Cefalo alone at the Miami 45. Cefalo raced the rest of the way untouched, completing a 76-yard touchdown play. After an exchange of field goals in the second period, Washington tied the game when quarterback Joe Theismann threw a four-yard touchdown pass to wide receiver Alvin Garrett. Miami immediately regained the lead when Fulton Walker took Jeff Hayes' kickoff and raced 98 yards for a touchdown, the first kickoff return for a score in Super Bowl history.

Miami led 17–10 at halftime, despite having been outgained 191 yards to 142. But the Dolphins' day was over. They gained only 34 yards in the second half, including none on 11 pass attempts.

The Redskins cut the margin to 17–13 in the third quarter, and then in the fourth, the Hogs began to dominate the Killer Bees. Faced with a fourth-and-one at the Miami 43, the Redskins sent Riggins around left end. He shed a tackle attempt by cornerback Don McNeal and lumbered 43 yards for the go-ahead score. On the next drive, Washington clinched the game. Riggins, who was selected the game's most valuable player, carried the ball eight times before Theismann capped the day's scoring with a six-yard pass to wide receiver Charlie Brown.

SUPER BOWL XVIII

Los Angeles Raiders 38, Washington 9
Tampa Stadium
22 January 1984

Marcus Allen, Michael Zagaris/NFL Photos.

The Los Angeles defense shut down the most-prolific offense in NFL history, and Marcus Allen rushed for a Super Bowl-record 191 yards, as the Raiders smashed the Washington Redskins 38–9.

Early in the game, after Washington's first possession, the Raiders' Derrick Jensen broke through the Redskins' line, blocked Jeff Hayes' punt, and recovered it in the end zone to give Los Angeles a 7–0 advantage.

In the second quarter, Raiders' quarterback Jim Plunkett came out throwing. First he passed 50 yards to wide receiver Cliff Branch. Then, two plays later, he found Branch again, for a 12-yard touchdown and a 14–0 lead. Washington responded with only a field goal.

The big play of the game came shortly before halftime. The Redskins had the ball on their own 12 with 12 seconds left in the half. Quarterback Joe Theismann called a swing pass to running back Joe Washington. Jack Squirek intercepted, and dashed into the end zone for a touchdown and a 21–3 halftime lead.

The Redskins opened the second half with a 70-yard touchdown drive, but their momentum immediately disappeared when Don Hasselbeck blocked the extra-point attempt. The Raiders responded with an eight-play, 78-yard drive, which was capped by a five-yard touchdown run by running back Marcus Allen.

On the last play of the third quarter, Allen struck again. On first-and-10 at the Raiders' 26, he took a pitch, swept left, reversed his direction, circled back to the middle, and cut upfield. Suddenly, he was in the open and a 74-yard touchdown run, the longest in Super Bowl history.

SUPER BOWL XIX

San Francisco 38, Miami 16
Stanford Stadium
20 January 1985

Roger Craig, John McDonough/NFL Photos.

Marino completed four of five passes as the Dolphins took a 3–0 lead on their first possession.

The 49ers responded with Montana nickle-and-diming his way downfield until he hit reserve running back Carl Monroe with a 33-yard touchdown pass. On the drive, Montana showed the major difference between him and the relatively immobile Marino, when he ran 15 yards for a first down on third-and-seven.

Miami quickly moved 70 yards in six plays without a huddle, scoring on a two-yard pass to tight end Dan Johnson. But Marino's lightning-quick strike forced the 49ers' coaches to put in a new 4–2–5 defense which featured six defensive backs and concentrated on stopping Miami's short passes. It worked so well that Marino, who had completed 9 of his first 10 passes, did not complete another until less than two minutes remained in the first half. By that time the game was all but over.

In the second quarter, the 49ers scored three touchdowns. The first was on an eight-yard pass from Montana to running back Roger Craig; the second on a six-yard run by Montana; and the third was scored on Craig's two-yard run. Despite two field goals by Miami late in the half, the 49ers led 28–16 at intermission.

San Francisco controlled the second half, building its lead on Craig's record third touchdown. By the end of the game, the 49ers had gained a game-record 537 yards, with Montana, the game's most valuable player, passing for 331 and running for 59.

SUPER BOWL XX

Chicago 46, New England 10
Louisiana Superdome, New Orleans
26 January 1986

Michael Zagaris/NFL Photos.

The Patriots scored first, with Tony Franklin's 36-yard field goal.

The Bears stormed back. Kevin Butler kicked two field goals. On the Patriots' first play after the Bears' second field goal, running back Craig James fumbled and linebacker Mike Singletary recovered at the New England 13. On second down, running back Matt Suhey blasted 11 yards for a touchdown and a 13-3 Chicago lead.

Two long scoring drives – one ending in a two-yard touchdown run by quarterback Jim McMahon and the other with Butler's third field goal – built the Bears' lead to 23-3 at intermission.

The Bears ended any hopes the Patriots might have on their first play of the third quarter. With a first-and-10 from his own 4, McMahon passed 60 yards to wide receiver Willie Gault. Eight plays later, McMahon scored from the 1 for a 30-3 lead. Three plays later, the Bears' reserve cornerback Reggie Phillips intercepted a pass from quarterback Steve Grogan – who had relieved Eason – and returned it 28 yards for a touchdown.

Late in the third quarter, defensive tackle William (The Refrigerator) Perry was inserted at running back and banged into the end zone for a 44-3 lead. And in the fourth quarter, reserve defensive tackle Henry Waechter sacked Grogan for a safety. In recognition of the Bears' brilliant defensive effort, defensive end Richard Dent was named the game's most valuable player.

SUPER BOWL XXI

New York Giants 39, Denver 20
Rose Bowl, Pasadena
25 January 1987

Phil Simms, Bill Cummings
/NFL Photos.

The New York Giants exploded for 30 points in the second
half to break open a close game and bury Denver 39–20. It
was the first NFL title for the Giants since 1956.

Denver's Rich Karlis opened the scoring with a 48-yard
field goal. However, on the next series, New York drove 78
yards in nine plays, taking a 7–3 lead on quarterback Phil
Simms' six-yard touchdown pass to tight end Zeke
Mowatt. But the Broncos stormed right back with a
58-yard drive capped by quarterback John Elway's four-
yard run.

The Broncos had several chances to put the Giants away
in the second quarter. Once, with a first-and-goal at the
Giants' 1, they were held for three plays, following which
Karlis missed the field-goal attempt. Karlis also missed
another short field-goal try. The Giants cut the halftime
lead to a point when George Martin sacked Elway for a
safety.

The Giants took command of the game in the third
period, with the key play being a successful conversion of a
fourth-and-one situation in which the Giants faked a punt.
The drive ended with a 13-yard touchdown pass from
Simms to tight end Mark Bavaro. New York also scored on
a field goal and a one-yard run by running back Joe Morris
to take a 26–10 lead after three periods.

The Giants and Broncos traded scores in the final
period, including Simms' third touchdown pass of the day,
a six-yarder to wide receiver Phil McConkey. Simms was
named the game's most valuable player after setting Super
Bowl records for most consecutive completions (10) and
highest completion percentage (88 on 22 completions in 25
attempts).

SUPER BOWL XXII

Washington 42, Denver 10
San Diego Jack Murphy Stadium
31 January 1988

Ricky Sanders, Al Messerschmidt/NFL Photos.

The Washington Redskins used record-setting performances by quarterback Doug Williams and running back Timmy Smith and the most prolific quarter in Super Bowl history to propel them to a smashing 42–10 victory over the Denver Broncos.

Initially, the game appeared to be going totally in favor of the Broncos. On their first offensive play, quarterback John Elway threw a 56-yard touchdown pass to wide receiver Ricky Nattiel. Then, following a Washington punt, the Broncos moved 61 yards in six plays to set up a 24-yard field goal by Rich Karlis.

But everything changed in the second quarter, as the Redskins erupted for 35 points on five possessions, taking a total of only 18 plays. Williams was the key figure in the explosion, throwing four touchdown passes, of 80 and 50 yards to wide receiver Ricky Sanders, 27 yards to wide receiver Gary Clark, and 8 yards to tight end Clint Didier. The fifth score came on a 58-yard run by Smith.

The second half was relatively uneventful, with the only score coming in the fourth quarter on a four-yard run by Smith. Nevertheless, the Redskins' numbers were staggering. They set a Super Bowl record with 602 total yards. Smith broke Marcus Allen's game rushing record by gaining 204 yards on 22 carries. And Sanders broke Lynn Swann's receiving yardage record by making eight receptions for 193 yards.

The most impressive display, however, was by Williams, who was selected as the game's most valuable player. He completed 18 of 29 passes for a record 340 yards, and his four touchdowns in the second quarter equalled the most ever thrown in an entire Super Bowl previously.

SUPER BOWL XXIII

San Francisco 20, Cincinnati 16
Joe Robbie Stadium, Miami
22 January 1989

Jerry Rice, Tony Tomsic/NFL Photos.

In a strange game, the San Francisco 49ers dominated the Cincinnati Bengals on the field as well as statistically, but then needed some last-minute magic by Joe Montana.

Although the 49ers were clearly the dominant team in the first two periods, they continually self-destructed, and the 3–3 score at halftime was the first time in Super Bowl history that the score had been tied at the intermission. During that time, Mike Cofer kicked a 41-yard field goal for the 49ers, and Jim Breech matched it with a 34-yarder for the Bengals.

The two teams again traded field goals in the third quarter, before the scoreboard was suddenly lit up. After Cofer's 32-yard field goal had tied the score 6–6, the Bengals jumped ahead when Stanford Jennings returned the kickoff 93 yards for a touchdown with 34 seconds remaining in the third quarter.

The 49ers wasted no time in tying the score again. Quarterback Joe Montana took his team 85 yards in only four plays, the 14-yard scoring pass to wide receiver Jerry Rice coming just 57 seconds into the fourth quarter. The score remained tied until only 3:20 remained, when Breech kicked his third field goal of the day, a 40-yarder.

The 49ers started their winning drive at their own 8, but never doubted the magic of Montana. On the drive's eleventh play, with only 34 seconds remaining, he threw 10 yards to wide receiver John Taylor for the winning touchdown. On the day, Montana completed 23 of 36 passes for a Super Bowl record 357 yards and two touchdowns. However, most valuable player honors were awarded to Rice, who caught 11 passes for a Super Bowl record 215 yards.

SUPER BOWL XXIV

San Francisco 55, Denver 10
Louisiana Superdome, New Orleans
28 January 1990

Ronnie Lott, Michael Zagaris/NFL Photos.

In the most one-sided Super Bowl in history, the San Francisco 49ers ran up the score on an outmanned Denver team, whose defense against the pass never materialized in a 55–10 thrashing.

The 49ers scored touchdowns on four of their six first-half possessions, three coming on touchdown passes by quarterback Joe Montana. First, Montana connected with wide receiver Jerry Rice for a 20-yard score. Then, after Denver's David Treadwell kicked a 42-yard field goal, Montana ended a 54-yard drive with a seven-yard pass to tight end Brent Jones. In the second quarter, fullback Tom Rathman culminated a 69-yard drive with a one-yard run. Montana's pass to Rice for 38 yards and another touchdown made the margin 27–3 at halftime.

49ers' offense kept firing on all cylinders. Montana found Rice for a record third touchdown reception – from 28 yards out – and then broke another Super Bowl record by throwing his fifth touchdown pass of the day, 35 yards to wide receiver John Taylor.

Elway's touchdown run of three yards near the end of the third quarter only seemed to encourage the 49ers to leave in their starters, who scored twice in the fourth quarter to give the game its final score, before the reserves took over.

Montana, who completed 22 of 29 passes for 297 yards and the five scores, was named the game's most valuable player for a record third time.

SUPER BOWL XXV

New York Giants 20, Buffalo 19
Tampa Stadium
27 January 1991

Thurman Thomas, Paul Spinelli/NFL Photos.

It was generally conceded that the New York Giants had to play a perfect game to have a chance of defeating Buffalo. But New York head coach Bill Parcells developed a brilliant game plan to maintain possession of the football and keep the Bills' high-powered offense off the field.

Early in the second quarter, the Bills appeared to take control of the game, driving 80 yards to a one-yard touchdown run by Don Smith. Buffalo increased its lead to 12–3 when defensive end Bruce Smith sacked Giants quarterback Jeff Hostetler – who was playing in place of the injured Phil Simms – for a safety.

But the Giants got back into the game on a 14-yard touchdown pass from Hostetler to wide receiver Stephen Baker only 25 seconds before halftime. The Giants dominated the third quarter, taking the second half kickoff and marching 75 yards to a go-ahead touchdown on a one-yard run by Ottis Anderson, the game's most valuable player. The drive took 9:29 off the clock and exhausted the Buffalo defense.

The Bills regained the lead on the first play of the fourth quarter. Halfback Thurman Thomas, who gained 135 yards rushing and 55 receiving during the day, raced 31 yards for a touchdown that made the score 19–17. But another time-consuming New York drive ended in a 21-yard field goal, and the Giants led 20–19.

After an exchange of punts, Buffalo took over deep in its own territory, and drove to the New York 30. But on the last play of the game, Scott Norwood's 47-yard field goal attempt was wide right, and the Giants had hung on.

NFL
CHAMPIONSHIP GAMES

Season	Date	Winner		Loser	
1932	Dec. 18	CHICAGO BEARS	9	Portsmouth	0
1933	Dec. 17	CHICAGO BEARS	23	N.Y. Giants	21
1934	Dec. 9	N.Y. GIANTS	30	Chi. Bears	13
1935	Dec. 15	DETROIT	26	N.Y. Giants	7
1936	Dec. 13	Green Bay	21	Boston	6
1937	Dec. 12	Washington	28	CHI. BEARS	21
1938	Dec. 11	N.Y. GIANTS	23	Green Bay	17
1939	Dec. 10	GREEN BAY	27	N.Y. Giants	0
1940	Dec. 8	Chi. Bears	73	WASHINGTON	0
1941	Dec. 21	CHI. BEARS	37	N.Y. Giants	9
1942	Dec. 13	WASHINGTON	14	Chi. Bears	6
1943	Dec. 26	CHI. BEARS	41	Washington	21
1944	Dec. 17	Green Bay	14	N.Y. GIANTS	7
1945	Dec. 16	CLEVELAND	15	Washington	14
1946	Dec. 15	Chi. Bears	24	N.Y. GIANTS	14
1947	Dec. 28	CHI. CARDINALS	28	Philadelphia	21
1948	Dec. 19	PHILADELPHIA	7	Chi. Cardinals	0
1949	Dec. 18	Philadelphia	14	L.A. RAMS	0
1950	Dec. 24	CLEVELAND	30	L.A. Rams	28
1951	Dec. 23	L.A. RAMS	24	Cleveland	17
1952	Dec. 28	Detroit	17	CLEVELAND	7
1953	Dec. 27	DETROIT	17	Cleveland	16
1954	Dec. 26	CLEVELAND	56	Detroit	10
1955	Dec. 26	Cleveland	38	L.A. RAMS	14
1956	Dec. 30	N.Y. GIANTS	47	Chi. Bears	7
1957	Dec. 29	DETROIT	59	Cleveland	14
1958	Dec. 28	Baltimore	23	N.Y. GIANTS	17*
1959	Dec. 27	BALTIMORE	31	N.Y. Giants	16
1960	Dec. 26	PHILADELPHIA	17	Green Bay	13
1961	Dec. 31	GREEN BAY	37	N.Y. Giants	0
1962	Dec. 30	Green Bay	16	N.Y. GIANTS	7
1963	Dec. 29	CHI. BEARS	14	N.Y. Giants	10
1964	Dec. 27	CLEVELAND	27	Baltimore	0
1965	Jan. 2	GREEN BAY	23	Cleveland	12
1966	Jan. 1	Green Bay	34	DALLAS	27
1967	Dec. 31	GREEN BAY	21	Dallas	17
1968	Dec. 29	Baltimore	34	CLEVELAND	0
1969	Jan. 4	MINNESOTA	27	Cleveland	7

AFL
CHAMPIONSHIP GAMES

Season	Date	Winner		Loser	
1960	Jan. 1	HOUSTON	24	L.A. Chargers	16
1961	Dec. 24	Houston	10	SAN DIEGO	3
1962	Dec. 23	Dallas	20	HOUSTON	17*
1963	Jan. 5	SAN DIEGO	51	Boston	10
1964	Dec. 26	BUFFALO	20	San Diego	7
1965	Dec. 26	Buffalo	23	SAN DIEGO	0
1966	Jan. 1	Kansas City	31	BUFFALO	7
1967	Dec. 31	OAKLAND	40	Houston	7
1968	Dec. 29	N.Y. JETS	27	Oakland	23
1969	Jan. 4	Kansas City	17	OAKLAND	7

NFC
CHAMPIONSHIP GAMES

Season	Date	Winner		Loser	
1970	Jan. 3	Dallas	17	SAN FRANCISCO	10
1971	Jan. 2	DALLAS	14	San Francisco	3
1972	Dec. 31	WASHINGTON	26	Dallas	3
1973	Dec. 30	Minnesota	27	DALLAS	10
1974	Dec. 29	MINNESOTA	14	L.A. Rams	10
1975	Jan. 4	Dallas	37	L.A. RAMS	7
1976	Dec. 26	MINNESOTA	24	L.A. Rams	13
1977	Jan. 1	DALLAS	23	Minnesota	6
1978	Jan. 7	Dallas	28	L.A. RAMS	0
1979	Jan. 6	L.A. Rams	9	TAMPA BAY	0
1980	Jan. 11	PHILADELPHIA	20	Dallas	7
1981	Jan. 10	SAN FRANCISCO	28	Dallas	27
1982	Jan. 23	WASHINGTON	31	Dallas	17
1983	Jan. 8	WASHINGTON	24	SAN FRANCISCO	21
1984	Jan. 6	SAN FRANCISCO	23	Chi. Bears	0
1985	Jan. 12	CHI. BEARS	24	L.A. Rams	0
1986	Jan. 11	N.Y. GIANTS	17	Washington	0
1987	Jan. 17	WASHINGTON	17	Minnesota	10
1988	Jan. 8	San Francisco	28	CHI. BEARS	3
1989	Jan. 14	SAN FRANCISCO	30	L.A. Rams	3
1990	Jan. 20	N.Y. Giants	15	SAN FRANCISCO	13

AFC
CHAMPIONSHIP GAMES

Season	Date	Winner		Loser	
1970	Jan. 3	BALTIMORE	27	Oakland	17
1971	Jan. 2	MIAMI	14	Baltimore	0
1972	Dec. 31	Miami	21	PITTSBURGH	17
1973	Dec. 30	MIAMI	27	Oakland	10
1974	Dec. 29	Pittsburgh	24	OAKLAND	13
1975	Jan. 4	PITTSBURGH	16	Oakland	10
1976	Dec. 26	OAKLAND	24	Pittsburgh	7
1977	Jan. 1	DENVER	20	Oakland	17
1978	Jan. 7	PITTSBURGH	34	Houston	5
1979	Jan. 6	PITTSBURGH	27	Houston	13
1980	Jan. 11	Oakland	34	SAN DIEGO	27
1981	Jan. 10	CINCINNATI	27	San Diego	7
1982	Jan. 22	MIAMI	14	N.Y. Jets	0
1983	Jan. 8	L.A. RAIDERS	30	Seattle	14
1984	Jan. 6	MIAMI	45	Pittsburgh	28
1985	Jan. 12	New England	31	MIAMI	14
1986	Jan. 11	Denver	23	CLEVELAND	20*
1987	Jan. 17	DENVER	38	Cleveland	33
1988	Jan. 8	CINCINNATI	21	Buffalo	10
1989	Jan. 14	DENVER	37	Cleveland	21
1990	Jan. 20	BUFFALO	51	L.A. Raiders	3

* Sudden-death overtime
CAPITALS indicate home team

PRO BOWL RESULTS

Date	Result	Site (attendance)
Jan 15, 1939	New York Giants 13, Pro All-Stars 10	Wrigley Field, Los Angeles (20,000)
Jan. 14, 1940	Green Bay 16, NFL All-Stars 7	Gilmore Stadium, Los Angeles (18,000)
Dec. 29, 1940	Chicago Bears, 28, NFL All-Stars 14	Gilmore Stadium, Los Angeles (21,624)
Jan. 4, 1942	Chicago Bears 35, NFL All-Stars 24	Polo Grounds, New York (17,725)
Dec. 27, 1942	NFL All-Stars 17, Washington 14	Shibe Park, Philadelphia (18,671)
Jan 14, 1951	American Conf. 28, National Conf. 27	Los Angeles Memorial Coliseum (53,676)
Jan 12, 1952	National Conf. 30, American Conf. 13	Los Angeles Memorial Coliseum (19,400)
Jan 10, 1953	National Conf. 27, American Conf. 7	Los Angeles Memorial Coliseum (34,208)
Jan 17, 1954	East 20, West 9	Los Angeles Memorial Coliseum (44,214)
Jan 16, 1955	West 26, East 19	Los Angeles Memorial Coliseum (43,972)
Jan 15, 1956	East 31, West 30	Los Angeles Memorial Coliseum (37,867)
Jan 13, 1957	West 19, East 10	Los Angeles Memorial Coliseum (44,177)
Jan 12, 1958	West 26, East 7	Los Angeles Memorial Coliseum (66,634)
Jan 11, 1959	East 28, West 21	Los Angeles Memorial Coliseum (72,250)
Jan 17, 1960	West 38, East 21	Los Angeles Memorial Coliseum (56,876)
Jan 15, 1961	West 35, East 31	Los Angeles Memorial Coliseum (62,971)
Jan 7, 1962	AFL West 47, East 27	Balboa Stadium, San Diego (20,973)
Jan 14, 1962	NFL West 31, East 30	Los Angeles Memorial Coliseum (57,409)
Jan 13, 1963	AFL West 21, East 14	Balboa Stadium, San Diego (27,641)
Jan 13, 1963	NFL East 30, West 20	Los Angeles Memorial Coliseum (61,374)
Jan 12, 1964	NFL West 31, East 17	Los Angeles Memorial Coliseum (67,242)
Jan 19, 1964	AFL West 27, East 24	Balboa Stadium, San Diego (20,016)
Jan 10, 1965	NFL West 34, East 14	Los Angeles Memorial Coliseum (60,598)
Jan 16, 1965	AFL West 38, East 14	Jeppesen Stadium, Houston (15,446)
Jan 15, 1966	AFL All-Stars 30, Buffalo 19	Rice Stadium, Houston (35,572)
Jan 15, 1966	NFL East 36, West 7	Los Angeles Memorial Coliseum (60,124)
Jan 21, 1967	AFL East 30, West 23	Oakland-Alameda County Coliseum (18,876)

Jan 22, 1967	NFL East 20, West 10	Los Angeles Memorial Coliseum (15,062)
Jan 21, 1968	AFL East 25, West 24	Gator Bowl, Jacksonville, Fla. (40,103)
Jan 21, 1968	NFL West 38, East 20	Los Angeles Memorial Coliseum (53,289)
Jan 19, 1969	AFL West 38, East 25	Gator Bowl, Jacksonville Fla. (41.058)
Jan 19, 1969	NFL West 10, East 7	Los Angeles Memorial Coliseum (32,050)
Jan 17, 1970	AFL West 26, East 3	Astrodome, Houston (30,170)
Jan 18, 1970	NFL West 16, East 13	Los Angeles Memorial Coliseum (57,786)
Jan 24, 1991	NFC 27, AFC 6	Los Angeles Memorial Coliseum (48,222)
Jan 23, 1972	AFC 26, NFC 13	Los Angeles Memorial Coliseum (53,647)
Jan 21, 1973	AFC 33, NFC 28	Texas Stadium, Irving (37,091)
Jan 20, 1974	AFC 15, NFC 13	Arrowhead Stadium, Kansas City (66,918)
Jan 20, 1975	NFC 17, AFC 10	Orange Bowl, Miami (26,484)
Jan 26, 1976	NFC 23, AFC 20	Louisiana Superdome, New Orleans (30,546)
Jan 17, 1977	AFC 24, NFC 14	Kingdome, Seattle (64,752)
Jan 23, 1978	NFC 14, AFC 13	Tampa Stadium (51,337)
Jan 29, 1979	NFC 13, AFC 7	Los Angeles Memorial Coliseum (46,281)
Jan 27, 1980	NFC 37, AFC 27	Aloha Stadium, Honolulu (49,800)
Jan 27, 1981	NFC 21, AFC 7	Aloha Stadium, Honolulu (50,360)
Jan 31, 1982	AFC 16, NFC 13	Aloha Stadium, Honolulu (50,402)
Feb 6, 1983	NFC 20, AFC 19	Aloha Stadium, Honolulu (49,883)
Jan 28, 1984	NFC 45, AFC 3	Aloha Stadium, Honolulu (50,445)
Jan 27, 1985	AFC 22, NFC 14	Aloha Stadium, Honolulu (50,385)
Feb 2, 1986	NFC 28, AFC 24	Aloha Stadium, Honolulu (50,101)
Feb 1, 1987	AFC 10, NFC 6	Aloha Stadium, Honolulu (50,101)
Feb 7, 1988	AFC 15, NFC 6	Aloha Stadium, Honolulu (50,113)
Jan 29, 1989	NFC 34, AFC 3	Aloha Stadium, Honolulu (50,113)
Feb 4, 1990	NFC 27, AFC 21	Aloha Stadium, Honolulu (50,445)
Feb 3, 1991	AFC 23, NFC 21	Aloha Stadium, Honolulu (50,345)

THE PRO FOOTBALL
HALL OF FAME

The Pro Football Hall of Fame is located in Canton, Ohio, site of the 1920 organizational meeting from which the NFL evolved. New members are elected annually by a 30-member national board of selectors, made up of media representatives from every league city, one at-large representative, and the president of the Pro Football Writers of America. Between four and seven new members are elected each year. An affirmative vote of approximately 80 percent is needed for election. Players must be retired five years to be eligible, while a coach need only be retired, with no time limit specified. Contributors (administrators, owners, etc.) may be elected while they are still active.

ROSTER OF MEMBERS

HERB ADDERLEY
Defensive back. 6-1, 200. Born in Philadelphia, Pennsylvania, June 8, 1939. Michigan State. Inducted in 1980. 1961-69 Green Bay Packers, 1970-72 Dallas Cowboys.

LANCE ALWORTH
Wide receiver. 6-0, 184. Born in Houston, Texas, August 13, 1940. Arkansas. Inducted in 1978. 1962-70 San Diego Chargers, 1971-72 Dallas Cowboys.

DOUG ATKINS
Defensive end. 6-8, 275. Born in Humboldt, Tennessee, May 8, 1930. Tennessee. Inducted in 1982. 1953-54 Cleveland Browns, 1955-66 Chicago Bears, 1967-69 New Orleans Saints.

MORRIS (RED) BADGRO
End. 6-0, 190. Born in Orilla, Washington, December 1, 1902. Southern California. Inducted in 1981. 1927 New York Yankees, 1930-35 New York Giants, 1936 Brooklyn Dodgers.

CLIFF BATTLES
Halfback. 6-1, 201. Born in Akron, Ohio, May 1, 1910. Died April 28, 1981. West Virginia Wesleyan. Inducted in 1968. 1932 Boston Braves, 1933-36 Boston Redskins, 1937 Washington Redskins.

SAMMY BAUGH
Quarterback. 6-2, 180. Born in Temple, Texas, March 17, 1914. Texas Christian. Inducted in 1963. 1937-52 Washington Redskins.

*Sammy Baugh, Pro Football Hall of Fame
/NFL Photos.*

CHUCK BEDNARIK
Center-linebacker. 6–3, 230. Born in Bethlehem,
Pennsylvania, May 1, 1925. Pennsylvania. Inducted in
1967. 1949–62 Philadelphia Eagles.

BERT BELL
Team owner. Commissioner. Born in Philadelphia,
Pennsylvania, February 25, 1895. Died October 11, 1959.
Pennsylvania. Inducted in 1963. 1933–40 Philadelphia
Eagles, 1941–42 Pittsburgh Steelers, 1943 Phil-Pitt,
1944–46 Pittsburgh Steelers. Commissioner, 1946–59.

BOBBY BELL
Linebacker. 6–4, 225. Born in Shelby, North Carolina,
June 17, 1940. Minnesota. Inducted in 1983. 1963–74
Kansas City Chiefs.

RAYMOND BERRY
End. 6–2, 187. Born in Corpus Christi, Texas, February
27, 1933. Southern Methodist. Inducted in 1973. 1955–67
Baltimore Colts.

CHARLES W. BIDWILL, SR.
Team owner. Born in Chicago, Illinois, September 16,
1895. Died April 19, 1947. Loyola of Chicago. Inducted in
1967. 1933–43 Chicago Cardinals, 1944 Card-Pitt, 1945–47
Chicago Cardinals.

FRED BILETNIKOFF
Wide receiver. 6–1, 190. Born in Erie, Pennsylvania,
February 23, 1943. Florida State. Inducted in 1988.
1965–78 Oakland Raiders.

GEORGE BLANDA
Quarterback-kicker. 6-2, 215. Born in Youngwood, Pennsylvania, September 17, 1927. Kentucky. Inducted in 1981. 1949–58 Chicago Bears, 1950 Baltimore Colts, 1960–66 Houston Oilers, 1967–75 Oakland Raiders.

MEL BLOUNT
Cornberback. 6-3, 205. Born in Vidalia, Georgia, April 10, 1948. Southern University. Inducted in 1989. 1970–83 Pittsburgh Steelers.

TERRY BRADSHAW
Quarterback. 6-3, 210. Born in Shreveport, Louisiana, September 2, 1948. Louisiana Tech. Inducted in 1989. 1970–83 Pittsburgh Steelers.

JIM BROWN
Fullback. 6-2, 232. Born in St. Simons, Georgia. February 17, 1936. Syracuse. Inducted in 1971. 1957–65 Cleveland Browns.

PAUL BROWN
Coach. Born in Norwalk, Ohio, September 7, 1908. Miami, Ohio. Inducted in 1967. 1946–49 Cleveland Browns (AAFC), 1950–62 Cleveland Browns, 1968–75 Cincinnati Bengals.

ROOSEVELT BROWN
Tackle. 6-3, 255. Born in Charlottesville, Virginia. October 20, 1932. Morgan State. Inducted in 1975. 1953–65 New York Giants.

WILLIE BROWN
Defensive back. 6-1, 210. Born in Yazoo City, Mississippi, December 2, 1940. Grambling. Inducted in 1984. 1963–66 Denver Broncos, 1967–78 Oakland Raiders.

Dick Butkus, Tony Tomsic/NFL Photos.

BUCK BUCHANAN
Defensive tackle. 6–7, 274. Born in Gainesville, Alabama, September 10, 1940. Grambling. Inducted in 1990. 1963–75 Kansas City Chiefs.

DICK BUTKUS
Linebacker. 6–3, 245. Born in Chicago, Illinois, December 9, 1942. Illinois. Inducted in 1979. 1965–73 Chicago Bears.

EARL CAMPBELL
Running back. 5–11, 233. Born in Tyler, Texas, March 29, 1955. Texas. Inducted in 1991. 1978–84 Houston Oilers, 1984–85 New Orleans Saints.

TONY CANADEO
Halfback. 5–11, 195. Born in Chicago, Illinois, May 5, 1919. Gonzaga. Inducted in 1974. 1941–44, 1946–52 Green Bay Packers.

JOE CARR
NFL president. Born in Columbus, Ohio, October 22, 1880. Died May 20, 1939. Did not attend college. Inducted in 1963. President, 1921–39 National Football League.

GUY CHAMBERLIN
End. Coach. 6–2, 210. Born in Blue Springs, Nebraska, January 16, 1894. Died April 4, 1967. Nebraska. Inducted in 1965. 1920 Decatur Staleys, 1921 Chicago Staleys, player-coach 1922–23 Canton Bulldogs, 1924 Cleveland Bulldogs, 1925–26 Frankford Yellow Jackets, 1927 Chicago Cardinals.

JACK CHRISTIANSEN
Defensive back. 6–1, 185. Born in Sublette, Kansas, December 20, 1928. Died June 29, 1986. Colorado State. Inducted in 1970. 1951–58 Detroit Lions.

EARL (DUTCH) CLARK
Quarterback. 6–0, 185. Born in Fowler, Colorado, October 11, 1906. Died August 5, 1978. Colorado College. Inducted in 1963. 1931–32 Portsmouth Spartans, 1934–38 Detroit Lions.

GEORGE CONNOR
Tackle-linebacker. 6–3, 240. Born in Chicago, Illinois, January 21, 1925. Holy Cross, Notre Dame. Inducted in 1975. 1948–55 Chicago Bears.

JIMMY CONZELMAN
Quarterback. Coach. Team Owner. 6–0, 180. Born in St. Louis, Missouri, March 6, 1898. Died July 31, 1970. Washington, Missouri. Inducted in 1964. 1920 Decatur Staleys, 1921–22 Rock Island, Ill. Independents, 1923–24 Milwaukee Badgers; owner-coach, 1925–26 Detroit Panthers; player-coach 1927–29, coach 1930 Providence

Steam Roller; coach, 1940–42 Chicago Cardinals, 1946–48 Chicago Cardinals.

LARRY CSONKA
Running back. 6–3, 235. Born in Stow, Ohio, December 25, 1946. Syracuse. Inducted in 1987. 1968–74, 1979 Miami Dolphins, 1976–78 New York Giants.

WILLIE DAVIS
Defensive end. 6–3, 245. Born in Lisbon, Louisiana, July 24, 1934. Grambling. Inducted in 1981. 1958–59 Cleveland Browns, 1960–69 Green Bay Packers.

LEN DAWSON
Quarterback. 6–0, 190. Born in Alliance, Ohio, June 20, 1935. Purdue. Inducted in 1987. 1957–59 Pittsburgh Steelers, 1960–61 Cleveland Browns, 1962 Dallas Texans, 1963–75 Kansas City Chiefs.

MIKE DITKA
Tight end. 6–3, 225. Born in Carnegie, Pennsylvania, October 18, 1939. Pittsburgh. Inducted in 1988. 1961–66 Chicago Bears, 1967–68 Philadelphia Eagles, 1969–72 Dallas Cowboys.

ART DONOVAN
Defensive tackle. 6–3, 265. Born in Bronx, New York, June 5, 1925. Boston College. Inducted in 1968. 1950 Baltimore Colts, 1951 New York Yanks, 1952 Dallas Texans, 1953–61 Baltimore Colts.

JOHN (PADDY) DRISCOLL
Quarterback. 5–11, 160. Born in Evanston, Illinois, January 11, 1896. Died June 29, 1968. Northwestern. Inducted in 1965. 1920 Decatur Staleys, 1920–25 Chicago Cardinals, 1926–29 Chicago Bears. Coach, 1956–57 Chicago Bears.

BILL DUDLEY
Halfback. 5–10, 176. Born in Bluefield, Virginia, December 24, 1921. Virginia. Inducted in 1966. 1942, 1945–46 Pittsburgh Steelers, 1947–49 Detroit Lions, 1950–51, 1953 Washington Redskins.

GLEN (TURK) EDWARDS
Tackle. 6–2, 260. Born in Mold, Washington, September 28, 1907. Died January 12, 1973. Washington State. Inducted in 1969. 1932 Boston Braves, 1933–36 Boston Redskins, 1937–40 Washington Redskins.

WEEB EWBANK
Coach. Born in Richmond, Indiana, May 6, 1907. Miami,
Ohio. Inducted in 19978. 1954–62 Baltimore Colts,
1963–73 New York Jets.

TOM FEARS
End. 6–2, 215. Born in Los Angeles, California, December
3, 1923. Santa Clara, UCLA. Inducted in 1970. 1948–56
Los Angeles Rams.

RAY FLAHERTY
End. Coach. Born in Spokane, Washington, September 1,
1904. Gonzaga. Inducted in 1976. 1926 Los Angeles
Wildcats (AFL), 1927–28 New York Yankees, 1928–29,
1931–35 New York Giants. Coach, 1936 Boston Redskins,
1937–42 Washington Redskins, 1946–48 New York
Yankees (AAFC), 1949 Chicago Hornets (AAFC).

LEN FORD
End. 6–5, 260. Born in Washington, D.C., February 18,
1926. Died March 14, 1972. Michigan. Inducted in 1976.
1948–49 Los Angeles Dons (AAFC) 1950–57 Cleveland
Browns, 1958 Green Bay Packers.

DAN FORTMANN
Guard. 6–0, 207. Born in Pearl River, New York, April 11,
1916. Colgate. Inducted in 1965. 1936–43 Chicago Bears.

FRANK GATSKI
Center. 6–3, 240. Born in Farmington, West Virginia,
March 18, 1922. Marshall, Auburn. Inducted in 1985.
1946–49 Cleveland Browns (AAFC), 1950–56 Cleveland
Browns, 1957 Detroit Lions.

BILL GEORGE
Linebacker. 6–2, 230. Born in Waynesburg, Pennsylvania,
October 27, 1930. Died September 30, 1982. Wake Forest.
Inducted in 1974. 1952–65 Chicago Bears, 1966 Los
Angeles Rams.

FRANK GIFFORD
Halfback. 6–1, 195. Born in Santa Monica, California,
August 16, 1930. Southern California. Inducted in 1977.
1952–60, 1962–64 New York Giants.

SID GILLMAN
Coach. Born in Minneapolis, Minnesota, October 26,
1911. Ohio State. Inducted in 1983. 1955–59 Los Angeles
Rams, 1960 Los Angeles Chargers, 1961–69 San Diego
Chargers, 1973–74 Houston Oilers.

Otto Graham, Frank Rippon/NFL Photos.

OTTO GRAHAM
Quarterback. 6–1, 195. Born in Waukegan, Illinois, December 6, 1921. Northwestern. Inducted in 1965. 1946–49 Cleveland Browns (AAFC), 1950–55 Cleveland Browns.

HAROLD (RED) GRANGE
Halfback. 6–0, 185. Born in Forksville, Pennsylvania, June 13, 1903. Illinois. Inducted in 1963. 1925 Chicago Bears, 1926 New York Yankees (AFL), 1927 New York Yankees, 1929–34 Chicago Bears.

JOE GREENE
Defensive tackle. 6–4, 260. Born in Temple, Texas, September 24, 1946. North Texas State. Inducted in 1987. 1969–81 Pittsburgh Steelers.

FORREST GREGG
Tackle. 6–4, 250. Born in Birthright, Texas, October 18, 1933. Southern Methodist. Inducted in 1977. 1956, 1958–70 Green Bay Packers, 1971 Dallas Cowboys.

BOB GRIESE
Quarterback. 6–1, 190. Born in Evansville, Indiana, February 3, 1945. Purdue. Inducted in 1990. 1967–80 Miami Dolphins.

LOU GROZA
Tackle-kicker. 6–3, 250. Born in Martin's Ferry, Ohio, January 25, 1924. Ohio State. Inducted in 1974. 1946–49 Cleveland Browns (AAFC), 1950–59, 1961–67 Cleveland Browns.

JOE GUYON
Halfback. 6–1, 180. Born in Mahnomen, Minnesota, November 26, 1892. Died November 27, 1971. Carlisle.

Georgia Tech. Inducted in 1966. 1920 Canton Bulldogs,
1921 Cleveland Indians, 1922–23 Oorang Indians, 1924
Rock Island, Ill, Independents, 1924–25 Kansas City
Cowboys, 1927 New York Giants.

GEORGE HALAS
End. Coach. Team owner. Born in Chicago, Illinois,
February 2, 1895. Died October 31, 1983. Illinois. Inducted
in 1963. 1920 Decatur Staleys, 1921 Chicago Staleys,
1922–29 Chicago Bears; coach, 1933–42, 1946–55, 1958–67
Chicago Bears.

George Halas, NFL Photos.

JACK HAM
Linebacker. 6–1, 225. Born in Johnstown, Pennsylvania,
December 23, 1948. Penn State. Inducted in 1988. 1971–82
Pittsburgh Steelers.

JOHN HANNAH
Guard. 6–3, 264. Born in Canton, Georgia, April 1, 1951.
Alabama. Inducted in 1991. 1973–85 New England
Patriots.

FRANCO HARRIS
Running back. 6–2, 225. Born in Fort Dix, New Jersey,
March 7, 1950. Penn State. Inducted in 1990. 1972–83
Pittsburgh Steelers, 1984 Seattle Seahawks.

ED HEALEY
Tackle. 6–3, 220. Born in Indian Orchard, Massachusetts,
December 28, 1894. Died December 9, 1978. Dartmouth.
Inducted in 1964. 1920–22 Rock Island, Ill., Independents,
1922–27 Chicago Bears.

MEL HEIN
Center 6–2, 225. Born in Redding, California, August 22,
!909. Washington State. Inducted in 1963. 1931–45 New
York Giants.

TED HENDRICKS
Linebacker. 6-7, 235. Born in Guatemala City,
Guatemala, November 1, 1947. Miami. Inducted in 1990.
1969-73 Baltimore Colts, 1974 Green Bay Packers,
1975-81 Oakland Raiders, 1982-83 Los Angeles Raiders.

WILBUR (PETE) HENRY
Tackle. 6-0, 250. Born in Mansfield, Ohio, October 31,
1897. Died February 7, 1952. Washington & Jefferson.
Inducted in 1963. 1920-23, 1925-26 Canton Bulldogs, 1927
New York Giants, 1927-28 Pottsville Maroons.

ARNIE HERBER
Quarterback. 6-1, 200. Born in Green Bay, Wisconsin,
April 2, 1910. Died October 14, 1969. Wisconsin, Regis
College. Inducted in 1966. 1930-40 Green Bay Packers,
1944-45 New York Giants.

BILL HEWITT
End. 5-11, 191. Born in Bay City, Michigan, October 8,
1909. Died January 14, 1947. Michigan. Inducted in 1971.
1932-36 Chicago Bears, 1937-39 Philadelphia Eagles, 1943
Phil-Pitt.

CLARKE HINKLE
Fullback. 5-11, 201. Born in Toronto, Ohio, April 10,
1909. Died November 9, 1988. Bucknell. Inducted in 1964.
1932-41 Green Bay Packers.

ELROY (CRAZYLEGS) HIRSCH
Halfback-end. 6-2, 190. Born in Wausau, Wisconsin, June
17, 1923. Wisconsin, Michigan. Inducted in 1968. 1946-48
Chicago Rockets (AAFC), 1949-57 Los Angeles Rams.

PAUL HORNUNG
Halfback. 6-2, 220. Born in Louisville, Kentucky,
December 23, 1935. Notre Dame. Inducted in 1986.
1957-62, 1964-66 Green Bay Packers.

KEN HOUSTON
Safety. 6-3, 198. Born in Lufkin, Texas, November 12,
1944. Prairie View A&M. Inducted in 1986. 1967-72
Houston Oilers, 1973-80 Washington Redskins.

CAL HUBBARD
Tackle. 6-5, 250. Born in Keytesville, Missouri, October
31, 1900. Died October 17, 1977. Centenary, Geneva.
Inducted in 1963. 1927-28 New York Giants, 1929-33, 1935
Green Bay Packers, 1936 New York Giants, 1936
Pittsburgh Pirates.

SAM HUFF
Linebacker, 6-1, 230. Born in Morgantown, West
Virginia, October 4, 1934. West Virginia. Inducted in 1982.

1956–63 New York Giants, 1964–67, 1969 Washington Redskins.

LAMAR HUNT
Team owner. Born in El Dorado, Arkansas, August 2, 1932. Southern Methodist. Inducted in 1972. 1960–62 Dallas Texans, 1963–90 Kansas City Chiefs.

DON HUTSON
End. 6–1, 180. Born in Pine Bluff, Arkansas, January 31, 1913. Alabama. Inducted in 1963. 1935–45 Green Bay Packers.

JOHN HENRY JOHNSON
Fullback. 6–2, 225. Born in Waterproof, Louisiana, November 24, 1929. St Mary's, Arizona State. Inducted in 1987. 1954–56 San Francisco 49ers, 1957–59 Detroit Lions, 1960–65 Pittsburgh Steelers, 1966 Houston Oilers.

DAVID (DEACON) JONES
Defensive end. 6–5, 250. Born in Eatonville, Florida, December 9, 1938. Mississippi Vocational. Inducted in 1980. 1961–71 Los Angeles Rams. 1972–73 San Diego Chargers, 1974 Washington Redskins.

STAN JONES
Guard-defensive tackle. 6–1, 250. Born in Altoona, Pennsylvania, November 24, 1931. Maryland. Inducted in 1991. 1954–65 Chicago Bears, 1966 Washington Redskins.

SONNY JURGENSEN
Quarterback. 6–0, 203. Born in Wilmington, North Carolina, August 23, 1934. Duke. Inducted in 1983. 1957–63 Philadelphia Eagles. 1964–74 Washington Redskins.

Senny Jergensen, Tony Tomsic/NFL Photos.

WALT KIESLING
Guard. Coach. 6-2, 245. Born in St Paul, Minnesota,
March 27, 1903. Died March 2, 1962. St Thomas
(Minnesota). Inducted in 1966. 1926-27 Duluth Eskimos,
1928 Pottsville Maroons, 1929-33 Chicago Cardinals, 1934
Chicago Bears, 1935-36 Green Bay Packers, 1937-38
Pittsburgh Pirates; coach, 1939-42 Pittsburgh Steelers; co-
coach, 1943 Phil-Pitt, 1944 Card-Pitt; coach, 1954-56
Pittsburgh Steelers.

FRANK (BRUISER) KINARD
Tackle. 6-1, 210. Born in Pelahatchie, Mississippi,
October 23, 1914. Died September 7, 1985. Mississippi.
Inducted in 1971. 1938-44 Brooklyn Dodgers-Tigers,
1946-47 New York Yankees (AAFC).

EARL (CURLY) LAMBEAU
Coach. Born in Green Bay. Wisconsin, April 9, 1898. Died
June 1, 1965, Notre Dame. Inducted in 1963. 1919-49
Green Bay Packers, 1950-51 Chicago Cardinals, 1952-53
Washington Redskins.

JACK LAMBERT
Linebacker. 6-4, 220 Born in Mantua, Ohio, July 8, 1952.
Kent State. Inducted in 1990. 1974-84 Pittsburgh Steelers.

TOM LANDRY
Coach. Born in Mission, Texas, September 11, 1924.
Texas. Inducted in 1990. 1960-88 Dallas Cowboys.

Tom Landry, John McDonough/NFL Photos.

DICK (NIGHT TRAIN) LANE
Defensive back. 6-2, 210. Born in Austin, Texas, April 16,
1928. Scottsbluff Junior College. Inducted in 1974.
1952-53 Los Angeles Rams, 1954-59 Chicago Cardinals,
1960-65 Detroit Lions.

JIM LANGER
Center. 6–2, 255. Born in Little Falls, Minnesota, May 16, 1948. South Dakota State. Inducted in 1987. Miami Dolphins 1970–79, 1980–81 Minnesota Vikings.

WILLIE LANIER
Linebacker. 6–1, 245. Born in Clover, Virginia, August 21, 1945. Morgan State. Inducted in 1986. 1967–77 Kansas City Chiefs.

YALE LARY
Defensive back-punter. 5–11. 189. Born in Fort Worth, Texas. November 24, 1930. Texas A&M. Inducted in 1 979. 1952–53, 1956–64 Detroit Lions.

DANTE LAVELLI
End. 6–0, 199. Born in Hudson, Ohio, February 23, 1923. Ohio State. Inducted in 1975. 1946–49 Cleveland Browns (AAFC), 1950–56 Cleveland Browns.

BOBBY LAYNE
Quarterback.6–2, 190. Born in Santa Anna, Texas, December 19, 1926. Died December 1, 1986. Texas. Inducted in 1967. 1948 Chicago Bears, 1949 New York Bulldogs, 1950–58 Detroit Lions, 1958–62 Pittsburgh Steelers.

ALPHONSE (TUFFY) LEEMANS
Fullback 6–0, 200. Born in Superior, Wisconsin, November 12, 1912. Died January 19, 1979. George Washington. Inducted in 1978. 1936–43 New York Giants.

BOB LILLY
Defensive tackle. 6–5, 260. Born in Olney, Texas, July 26, 1939. Texas Christian. Inducted in 1980. 1961–74 Dallas Cowboys.

Bob Lilly, Malcolm Emmons/NFL Photos.

VINCE LOMBARDI
Coach. Born in Brooklyn, New York, June 11, 1913. Died September 3, 1970. Fordham. Inducted in 1971. 1959-67 Green Bay Packers, 1969 Washington Redskins.

SID LUCKMAN
Quarterback. 6-0, 195. Born in Brooklyn, New York, November 21, 1916. Columbia. Inducted in 1965. 1939-50 Chicago Bears.

ROY (LINK) LYMAN
Tackle. 6-2, 252. Born in Table Rock, Nebraska, November 30, 1898. Died December 16, 1972. Nebraska. Inducted in 1964. 1922-23, 1925 Canton Bulldogs, 1924 Cleveland Bulldogs, 1925 Frankford Yellow Jackets, 1926-28, 1930-31, 1933-34 Chicago Bears.

TIM MARA
Team owner. Born in New York, New York, July 29, 1887. Died February 17, 1959. Did not attend college. Inducted in 1963. 1925-59 New York Giants.

GINO MARCHETTI
Defensive end. 6-4, 245. Born in Smithers, West Virginia, January 2, 1927. San Francisco. Inducted in 1972. 1952 Dallas Texans, 1953-64, 1966 Baltimore Colts.

GEORGE PRESTON MARSHALL
Team owner. Born in Grafton, West Virginia, October 11, 1897. Died August 9, 1969. Randolph-Macon. Inducted in 1963. 1932 Boston Braves, 1933-36 Boston Redskins, 1937-69 Washington Redskins.

OLLIE MATSON
Halfback. 6-2, 220. Born in Trinity, Texas, May 1, 1930. San Francisco. Inducted in 1972. 1952, 1954-58 Chicago Cardinals, 1959-62 Los Angeles Rans, 1963 Detroit Lions, 1964-66 Philadelphia Eagles.

DON MAYNARD
Wide receiver. 6-1, 175. Born in Crosbyton, Texas, January 25, 1935. Texas Western. Inducted in 1987. New York Giants 1958, New York Titans 1960-62, New York Jets 1963-72. St Louis Cardinals 1973.

GEORGE McAFFEE
Halfback. 6-0, 177. Born in Ironton, Ohio, March 13, 1918. Duke. Inducted in 1966. 1940-41, 1945-50 Chicago Bears.

MIKE McCORMACK
Tackle. 6-4, 248. Born in Chicago, Illinois, June 21, 1930. Kansas. Inducted in 1984. 1951 New York Yanks, 1954-62 Cleveland Browns.

HUGH McELHENNY
Halfback. 6-1, 198. Born in Los Angeles, California,
December 31, 1928. Washington. Inducted in 1970.
1952–60 San Francisco 49ers, 1961–62 Minnesota Vikings,
1963 New York Giants, 1964 Detroit Lions.

JOHNNY BLOOD (McNALLY)
Halfback. 6-0, 185. Born in New Richmond, Wisconsin,
November 27, 1903. Died November 28, 1985. St. John's
(Minnesota). Inducted in 1963. 1925–26 Milwaukee
Badgers, 1926–27 Duluth Eskimos, 1928 Pottsville
Maroons, 1929–33 Green Bay Packers, 1934 Pittsburgh
Pirates, 1935–36 Green Bay Packers; player-coach,
1937–39 Pittsburgh Pirates.

MIKE MICHALSKE
Guard. 6-0, 209. Born in Cleveland, Ohio, April 24, 1903.
Died October 26, 1983. Penn State. Inducted in 1964. 1926
New York Yankees (AFL), 1927–28 New York Yankees,
1929–35, 1937 Green Bay Packers.

WAYNE MILLNER
End. 6-0, 191. Born in Roxbury, Massachusetts, January
31, 1913. Died November 19, 1976. Notre Dame. Inducted
in 1968. 1936 Boston Redskins, 1937–42, 1945 Washington
Redskins.

BOBBY MITCHELL
Running back-wide receiver. 6-0, 195. Born in Hot
Springs, Arkansas, June 6, 1935. Illinois. Inducted in
1983. 1958–61 Cleveland Browns, 1962–68 Washington
Redskins.

RON MIX
Tackle. 6-4, 250. Born in Los Angeles, California, March
10, 1938. Southern California. Inducted in 1979. 1960 Los
Angeles Chargers, 1961–69 San Diego Chargers, 1971
Oakland Raiders.

LENNY MOORE
Back. 6-1, 198. Born in Reading, Pennsylvania,
November 25, 1933. Penn State. Inducted in 1975. 1956–67
Baltimore Colts.

MARION MOTLEY
Fullback. 6-1, 238. Born in Leesburg, Georgia, June 5,
1920. South Carolina State, Nevada. Inducted in 1968.
1946–49 Cleveland Browns (AAFC), 1950–53 Cleveland
Browns, 1955 Pittsburgh Steelers.

GEORGE MUSSO
Guard-tackle. 6-2, 270. Born in Collinsville, Illinois, April
8, 1910. Millikin. Inducted in 1982. 1933–44 Chicago
Bears.

BRONKO NAGURSKI
Fullback. 6–2, 225. Born in Rainy River, Ontario,
Canada, November 3, 1908. Died January 9, 1990.
Minnesota. Inducted in 1963. 1930–37, 1943 Chicago
Bears.

JOE NAMATH
Quarterback. 6–2, 200. Born in Beaver Falls,
Pennsylvania, May 31, 1943. Alabama. Inducted in 1985.
1965–76 New York Jets, 1977 Los Angeles Rams.

EARLE (GREASY) NEALE
Coach. Born in Parkersburg, West Virginia, November 5,
1891. Died November 2, 1973. West Virginia Wesleyan.
Inducted in 1969. 1941–42, 1944–50 Philadelphia Eagles,
co-coach, Phil-Pitt 1943.

ERNIE NEVERS
Fullback. 6–1, 205. Born in Willow River, Minnesota,
June 11, 1903. Died May 3, 1976. Stanford. Inducted in
1963. 1926–27 Duluth Eskimos, 1929–31 Chicago
Cardinals.

RAY NITSCHKE
Linebacker. 6–3, 235. Born in Elmwood Park, Illinois,
December 29, 1936. Illinois. Inducted in 1978. 1958–72
Green Bay Packers.

LEO NOMELLINI
Defense tackle. 6–3, 250. Born in Lucca, Italy, June 19,
1924. Minnesota. Inducted in 1969. 1950–63 San Francisco
49ers.

MERLIN OLSEN
Defensive tackle. 6–5, 270. Born in Logan, Utah,
September 15 1940. Utah State. Inducted in 1982. 1962–76
Los Angeles Rams.

Merlin Olson, Carl Skalak/NFL Photos.

JIM OTTO
Center. 6–2, 255. Born in Wausau, Wisconsin, January 5, 1938. Miami. Inducted in 1980. 1960–74 Oakland Raiders.

STEVE OWEN
Tackle. Coach. 6–0, 235. Born in Cleo Springs, Oklahoma, April 21, 1898. Died May 17, 1964. Phillips. Inducted in 1966. 1924–25 Kansas City Cowboys, 1926–30 New York Giants; coach, 1931–53 New York Giants.

ALAN PAGE
Defensive tackle. 6–4, 225. Born in Canton, Ohio, August 7, 1945. Inducted in 1988. 1967–78 Minnesota Vikings, 1978–81 Chicago Bears.

CLARENCE (ACE) PARKER
Quarterback. 5–11, 168. Born in Portsmouth, Virginia, May 17, 1912. Duke. Inducted in 1972. 1937–41 Brooklyn Dodgers, 1945 Boston Yanks, 1946 New York Yankees (AAFC).

JIM PARKER
Guard-tackle. 6–3, 273. Born in Macon, Georgia, April 3, 1934. Ohio State. Inducted in 1973. 1957–67 Baltimore Colts.

JOE PERRY
Fullback. 6–0, 200. Born in Stevens, Arkansas, January 22, 1927. Compton Junior College. Inducted in 1969. 1948–49 San Francisco 49ers (AAFC), 1950–60, 1963 San Francisco 49ers, 1961–62 Baltimore Colts.

PETE PIHOS
End. 6–1, 210. Born in Orlando, Florida, October 22, 1923. Indiana. Inducted in 1970. 1947–55 Philadelphia Eagles.

HUGH (SHORTY) RAY
Supervisor of officials 1938–56. Born in Highland Park, Illinois, September 21, 1884. Died September 16, 1956. Illinois. Inducted in 1966.

DAN REEVES
Team owner. Born in New York, New York, June 30, 1912. Died April 15, 1971. Georgetown. Inducted in 1967. 1941–45. Cleveland Rams, 1946–71 Los Angeles Rams.

JIM RINGO
Center, 6–1, 235. Born in Orange, New Jersey, November 21, 1931. Syracuse. Inducted in 1981. 1953–63 Green Bay Packers, 1964–67 Philadelphia Eagles.

ANDY ROBUSTELLI
Defensive end. 6–0, 230. Born in Stamford, Connecticut, December 6, 1925. Arnold College. Inducted in 1971. 1951–55 Los Angeles Rams, 1956–64 New York Giants.

ART ROONEY
Team owner. Born in Coulterville, Pennsylvania, January 27, 1901. Died August 25, 1988. Georgetown, Duquesne. Inducted in 1964. 1933–40 Pittsburgh Pirates, 1941–42, 1945–88 Pittsburgh Steelers, 1943 Phil-Pitt, 1944 Card-Pitt.

PETE ROZELLE
Commissioner. Born in South Gate, California, March 1, 1926. San Francisco. Inducted in 1985. Commissioner 1960–89.

BOB ST. CLAIR
Tackle. 6–9, 265. Born in San Francisco, California, February 18, 1931. San Francisco, Tulsa. Inducted in 1990. 1953–63 San Francisco 49ers.

GALE SAYERS
Running back. 6–0, 200. Born in Wichita, Kansas, May 30, 1943. Kansas. Inducted in 1977. 1965–71 Chicago Bears.

JOE SCHMIDT
Linebacker. 6–0, 222. Born in Pittsburgh, Pennsylvania, January 19, 1932. Pittsburgh. Inducted in 1973. 1953–65 Detroit Lions.

TEX SCHRAMM
Team president. Born in San Gabriel, California, June 2, 1920. Texas. Inducted 1991. 1960–88 Dallas Cowboys.

ART SHELL
Tackle. 6–5, 285. Born in Charleston, South Carolina, November 25, 1946. Maryland State-Eastern Shore. Inducted in 1989. 1968–81 Oakland Raiders, 1982 Los Angeles Raiders.

O. J. SIMPSON
Running back. 6–1, 212. Born in San Francisco, California, July 9, 1947. Southern California. Inducted in 1985. 1969–77 Buffalo Bills, 1978–79 San Francisco 49ers.

BART STARR
Quarterback. 6–1, 200. Born in Montgomery, Alabama, January 9, 1934. Alabama. Inducted in 1977. 1956–71 Green Bay Packers.

ROGER STAUBACH
Quarterback. 6–3, 202. Born in Cincinnati, Ohio, February, 5, 1942. Navy. Inducted in 1985. 1969–79 Dallas Cowboys.

ERNIE STAUTNER
Defensive tackle. 6–2, 235. Born in Prinzing-by-Cham, Bavaria, Germany, Aril 20, 1925. Boston College. Inducted in 1969. 1950–63 Pittsburgh Steelers.

JAN STENERUD
Kicker. 6-2, 187. Born in Fetsund, Norway, November 26, 1942. Montana State. Inducted in 1991. 1967–79 Kansas City Chiefs, 1980–83 Green Bay Packers, 1984–85 Minnesota Vikings.

KEN STRONG
Halfback. 5-11, 210. Born in New Haven, Connecticut, August 6, 1906. Died October 5, 1979. New York University. Inducted in 1967. 1929–32 Staten Island Stapletons, 1933–35, 1939, 1944–47 New York Giants, 1936–37 New York Yanks (AFL).

JOE STYDAHAR
Tackle. 6-4, 230. Born in Kaylor, Pennsylvania, March 3, 1912. Died March 23, 1977. West Virginia. Inducted in 1967. 1936–42, 1945–46 Chicago Bears.

FRANK TARKENTON
Quarterback. 6-0, 185. Born in Richmond, Virginia, February 3, 1940. Georgia. Inducted in 1986. 1961–66, 1972–78 Minnesota Vikings, 1967–71 New York Giants.

CHARLEY TAYLOR
Running back-wide receiver. 6-3, 210. Born in Grand Prairie, Texas, September 28, 1941. Arizona State. Inducted in 1984. 1964–75, 1977 Washington Redskins.

JIM TAYLOR
Fullback. 6-0, 216. Born in Baton Rouge, Louisiana, September 20, 1935. Louisiana State. Inducted in 1976. 1958–66 Green Bay Packers, 1967 New Orleans Saints.

JIM THORPE
Halfback. 6-1, 190. Born in Prague, Oklahoma, May 28, 1888. Died March 28, 1953. Carlisle. Inducted in 1963. 1915–17, 1919–20, 1926 Canton Bulldogs, 1921 Cleveland Indians, 1922–23 Oorang Indians, 1924 Rock Island, Ill., Independents, 1925 New York Giants, 1928 Chicago Cardinals.

Y.A. TITTLE
Quarterback. 6-0, 200. Born in Marshall, Texas, October 24, 1926. Louisiana State. Inducted in 1971. 1948–49 Baltimore Colts (AAFC), 1950 Baltimore Colts, 1951–60 San Francisco 49ers, 1961–64 New York Giants.

GEORGE TRAFTON
Center. 6-2, 235. Born in Chicago, Illinois, December 6, 1896. Died September 5, 1971. Notre Dame. Inducted in 1964. 1920 Decatur Staleys, 1921 Chicago Staleys, 1922–32 Chicago Bears.

CHARLEY TRIPPI
Halfback. 6–0, 185. Born in Pittston, Pennsylvania,
December 14, 1922. Georgie. Inducted in 1968. 1947–55
Chicago Cardinals.

EMLEN TUNNELL
Safety. 6–1, 200. Born in Bryn Mawr, Pennsylvania,
March 29, 1925. Died July 23, 1975. Toledo, Iowa.
Inducted in 1967. 1948–58 New York Giants, 1959–61
Green Bay Packers.

CLYDE (BULLDOG) TURNER
Center 6–2, 235. Born in Sweetwater. Texas, November 10,
1919. Hardin-Simmons. Inducted in 1966. 1940–52
Chicago Bears.

JOHNNY UNITAS
Quarterback. 6–1, 195. Born in Pittsburgh, Pennsylvania,
May 7, 1933. Louisville. Inducted in 1979. 1956–72
Baltimore Colts, 1973 San Diego Chargers.

GENE UPSHAW
Guard. 6–5, 255. Born in Robstown, Texas, August 15,
1945. Texas A&I. Inducted in 1987. 1967–81 Oakland
Raiders.

NORM VAN BROCKLIN
Quarterback, 6–1. 190. Born in Eagle Butte, South
Dakota, March 15, 1926. Died May 2, 1983. Oregon.
Inducted in 1971. 1949–57 Los Angeles Rams. 1958–60
Philadelphia Eagles.

STEVE VAN BUREN
Halfback. 6–1, 200. Born in La Ceiba, Honduras,
December 28, 1920. Louisiana State. Inducted in 1965.
1944–51 Philadelphia Eagles.

DOAK WALKER
Halfback. 5–10, 172. Born in Dallas, Texas, January 1,
1927. Southern Methodist. Inducted in 1986. 1950–55
Detroit Lions.

PAUL WARFIELD
Wide receiver. 6–0, 188. Born in Warren, Ohio, November
28, 1942. Ohio State. Inducted in 1983. 1964–69, 1976–77
Cleveland Browns, 1970–74 Miami Dolphins.

BOB WATERFIELD
Quarterback. 6–2, 200. Born in Elmira, New York, July
26, 1920. Died March 25, 1983. UCLA. Inducted in 1965.
1945 Cleveland Rams. 1946–52 Los Angeles Rams.

ARNIE WEINMEISTER
Defensive tackle. 6-4, 235. Born in Rhein, Saskatchewan, Canada, March 23, 1923. Washington. Inducted in 1984. 1948-49 New York Yankees (AAFC), 1950-53 New York Giants.

BILL WILLIS
Guard. 6-2, 215. Born in Columbus, Ohio, October 5, 1921. Ohio State. Inducted in 1977. 1946-49 Cleveland Browns (AAFC), 1950-53 Cleveland Browns.

LARRY WILSON
Safety. 6-0, 190. Born in Rigby, Idaho, March 24, 1938. Utah. Inducted in 1978. 1960-72 St. Louis Cardinals.

Larry Wilson, Tony Tomsic/NFL Photos.

ALEX WOJCIECHOWICZ
Center. 6-0, 235. Born in South River, New Jersey, August 12, 1915. Fordham. Inducted in 1968. 1938-46 Detroit Lions, 1946-50 Philadelphia Eagles.

WILLIE WOOD
Safety. 5-10, 190. Born in Washington, D.C., December 23, 1936. Southern California. Inducted in 1989. 1960-71 Green Bay Packers.

ALL-TIME RECORDS

SERVICE
Most Seasons
    26 George Blanda, Chi. Bears 1949, 1950–58;
        Baltimore 1950; Houston 1960–66; Oakland
        1967–75.

Most Seasons, One Club
    19 Jim Marshall, Minnesota 1961–79.

Most Games Played, Career
    340 George Blanda, Chi. Bears 1949, 1950–58;
        Baltimore 1950; Houston 1960–66; Oakland
        1967–75.

Most Consecutive Games Played
    282 Jim Marshall, Cleveland 1960; Minnesota
        1961–79.

SCORING
Most Seasons Leading League
    5 Don Hutson, Green Bay 1940–44.
    5 Gino Cappelletti, Boston 1961, 1963–66.

Most Consecutive Seasons Leading League
    5 Don Hutson, Green Bay 1940–44.

Most Points, Career
  2,002 George Blanda, Chi. Bears 1949, 1950–58;
        Baltimore 1950; Houston 1960–66; Oakland
        1967–75

Most Points, Season
    176 Paul Hornung, Green Bay 1960 (15 td, 41 pat, 15
        fg).

Most Points, No Touchdowns, Season
    161 Mark Moseley, Washington 1983 (62 pat, 33fg).

Most Seasons, 100 or More Points
    8 Nick Lowery, Kansas City 1981, 1983–86,
        1988–90.

Most Points, Game
    40 Ernie Nevers, Chi. Cardinals vs. Chi. Bears, 28
        Nov. 1929 (6td, 4 pat).

Most Consecutive Games Scoring
    151 Fred Cox, Minnesota 1963–73.

Most Touchdowns, Career
    126 Jim Brown, Cleveland 1957–65 (106 ru, 20 rec).

Jim Brown, Tony Tomsic/NFL Photos.

Most Touchdowns, Season
24 John Riggins, Washington 1983 (24 ru).

Most Touchdowns, Game
6 Ernie Nevers, Chi. Cardinals vs. Chi. Bears, 28 Nov. 1929 (6 ru).
6 Dub Jones, Cleveland vs. Chi. Bears, 25 Nov. 1951 (4 ru, 2 rec).
6 Gale Sayers, Chi. Bears vs. San Francisco, 12 Dec, 1965 (4 ru, 1 rec, 1 ret).

Most Consecutive Games Scoring Touchdowns
18 Lenny Moore, Baltimore 1963–65.

Most Points After Touchdown, Career
943 George Blanda, Chi. Bears 1949, 1950–58; Baltimore 1950; Houston 1960–66; Oakland 1967–75 (959 att).

Most Points After Touchdown, Season
66 Uwe von Schamann, Miami 1984 (70 att).

Most Points After Touchdown, Game
9 Pat Harder, Chi. Cardinals vs. N.Y. Giants, 17 Oct. 1948 (9 att).
9 Bob Waterfield, L.A. Rams vs. Baltimore, 22 Oct. 1950 (9 att).
9 Charlie Gogolak, Washington vs. N.Y. Giants, 27 Nov. 1966 (10 att).

Most Consecutive Points After Touchdown
234 Tommy Davis, San Francisco 1959–65.

Most Field Goals, Career
373 Jan Stenerud, Kansas City 1967–79; Green Bay 1980–83; Minnesota 1984–85 (558 att).

Most Field Goals, Season
     35 Ali Haji-Sheikh, N.Y. Giants 1983 (42 att).

Most Field Goals, Game
     7 Jim Bakken, St. Louis vs. Pittsburgh, 24 Sept.
        1967 (9 att).
     7 Rich Karlis, Minnesota vs. L.A. Rams, 5 Nov.
        1989 (7 att).

Most Consecutive Field Goals
     24 Kevin Butler, Chi. Bears 1988–89.

Most Consecutive Games Scoring Field Goals
     31 Fred Cox, Minnesota 1968–70.

Most Safeties, Career
     4 Ted Hendricks, Baltimore 1969–73; Green Bay
        1974; Oakland 1975–81; L.A. Raiders 1982–83.
     4 Doug English, Detroit 1975–79, 1981–85.

Most Safeties, Season
     2 By 11 Players.

Most Safeties, Game
     2 Fred Dryer, L.A. Rams vs. Green Bay, 21 Oct.
        1973.

RUSHING

Most Seasons Leading League
     8 Jim Brown, Cleveland 1957–61, 1963–65.

Most Consecutive Seasons Leading League
     5 Jim Brown, Cleveland 1957–61.

Most Attempts, Career
   3,838 Walter Payton, Chi. Bears 1975–87.

Most Attempts, Season
     407 James Wilder, Tampa Bay 1984.

Eric Dickerson, Peter Groh/NFL Photos.

Most Attempts, Game
45 Jamie Morris, Washington vs. Cincinnati, 17 Dec. 1988.

Most Yards Gained, Career
16,726 Walter Payton, Chi. Bears 1975–87.

Most Yards Gained, Season
2,105 Eric Dickerson, L.A. Rams 1984.

Most Yards Gained, Game
275 Walter Payton, Chi. Bears vs. Minnesota, 20 Nov. 1977.

Most Seasons, 1,000 or More Yards
10 Walter Payton, Chi. Bears 1976–81, 1983–86.

Most Games, 200 or More Yards
6 O. J. Simpson, Buffalo 1969–77; San Francisco 1978–79.

Most Games, 100 or More Yards
77 Walter Payton, Chi. Bears 1975–87.

Longest Run From Scrimmage
99 Tony Dorsett, Dallas vs. Minnesota, 3 Jan. 1983.

Tony Dorsett, PRM/NFL Photos.

Highest Average Gain, Career
5.22 Jim Brown, Cleveland 1957–65 (2,359–12,312).

Highest Average Gain, Season
9.94 Beattie Feathers, Chi. Bears 1934 (101–1,004).

Most Touchdowns, Career
110 Walter Payton, Chi. Bears 1975–87.

Most Touchdowns, Season
24 John Riggins, Washington 1983.

Most Touchdowns, Game
6 Ernie Nevers, Chi. Cardinals vs. Chi. Bears, 28 Nov. 1929.

Most Consecutive Games Rushing for Touchdowns
13 John Riggins, Washington 1982–83.
13 George Rogers, Washington 1985–86.

PASSING

Most Seasons Leading League
6 Sammy Baugh, Washington 1937, 1940, 1943, 1945, 1947, 1949.

Most Consecutive Seasons Leading League
2 By four players.

Highest Pass Rating, Career
93.4 Joe Montana, San Francisco 1979–90.

Highest Pass Rating, Season
112.4 Joe Montana, San Francisco 1989.

Most Attempts, Career
6,467 Fran Tarkenton, Minnesota 1961–66, 1972–78; N.Y. Giants 1967–71.

Most Attempts, Season
623 Dan Marino, Miami 1986.

Dan Marino, Bob Rosato/NFL Photos.

Most Attempts, Game
68 George Blanda, Houston vs. Buffalo, 1 Nov. 1964.

Most Completions, Career
3,686 Fran Tarkenton, Minnesota 1961–66, 1972–78;
N.Y. Giants 1967–71.

Most Completions, Season
378 Dan Marino, Miami 1986.

Most Completions, Game
42 Richard Todd, N.Y. Jets vs. San Francisco, 21
Sept. 1980.

Most Consecutive Completions
22 Joe Montana, San Francisco vs. Cleveland (5), 29
Nov. 1987; vs. Green Bay (17), 6 Dec. 1987.

Highest Completion Percentage, Career
63.64 Joe Montana, San Francisco 1978–90
(4,579–2,914).

Highest Completion Percentage, Season
70.55 Ken Anderson, Cincinnati 1982 (309–218).

Most Yards Gained, Career
47,003 Fran Tarkenton, Minnesota 1961–66, 1972–78;
N.Y. Giants 1967–71.

Most Yards Gained, Season
5,084 Dan Marino, Miami 1984.

Most Yards Gained, Game
554 Norm Van Brocklin, L.A Rams vs. N.Y. Yanks, 28
Sept. 1951.

Longest Pass from Scrimmage
99 Achieved 6 times.

Most Touchdown Passes, Career
342 Fran Tarkenton, Minnesota 1961–66, 1972–78;
N.Y. Giants 1967–71.

Johny Unitas, Malcolm Emmons/NFL Photos.

Most Touchdown Passes, Season
48 Dan Marino, Miami 1984

Most Touchdown Passes, Game
7 By five players.

Most Consecutive Games, Touchdown Passes
47 Johnny Unitas, Baltimore 1956–60.

PASS RECEIVING
Most Seasons Leading League
8 Don Hutson, Green Bay 1936–37, 1939, 1941–45.

Most Consecutive Seasons Leading League
5 Don Hutson, Green Bay 1941–45.

Most Pass Receptions, Career
819 Steve Largent, Seattle 1976–89.

Most Pass Receptions, Season
106 Art Monk, Washington 1984.

Art Monk, Arthur Anderson/NFL Photos.

Most Pass Receptions, Game
18 Tom Fears, L.A. Rams vs. Green Bay, 3 Dec.
1950.

Most Consecutive Games, Pass Receptions
177 Steve Largent, Seattle 1977–89.

Most Yards Gained, Career
13,089 Steve Largent, Seattle 1976–89.

Most Yards Gained, Season
1,746 Charley Hennigan, Houston 1961.

Most Yards Gained, Game
336 Willie (Flipper) Anderson, L.A. Rams vs. New
Orleans, 26 Nov. 1989.

Most Seasons, 1,000 or More Yards
8 Steve Largent, Seattle 1978-81, 1983-86.

Most Games, 200 or More Yards
5 Lance Alworth, San Diego 1962-70; Dallas 1971-72.

Most Games, 100 or More Yards
50 Don Maynard, N.Y. Giants 1958; N.Y. Titans 1960-62; N.Y. Jets 1963-72; St. Louis 1973.

Most Touchdowns, Career
100 Steve Largent, Seattle 1976-89.

Most Touchdowns, Season
22 Jerry Rice, San Francisco 1987.

Jerry Rice, Michael Zagaris/NFL Photos.

Most Touchdowns, Game
5 Bob Shaw, Chi. Cardinals vs. Baltimore, 2 Oct. 1950.
5 Kellen Winslow, San Diego vs. Oakland, 22 Nov. 1981.
5 Jerry Rice, San Francisco vs. Atlanta, 14 Oct. 1990.

Most Consecutive Games, Touchdowns
13 Jerry Rice, San Francisco 1986-87.

ALL-TIME
LEADING RUSHERS

Walter Payton, Ron Vesely/NFL Photos.

	Yrs.	Att.	Yards	Avg.	TD
1. Walter Payton	13	3,838	16,726	4.4	110
2. Tony Dorsett	12	2,936	12,739	4.3	77
3. Jim Brown	9	2,359	12,312	5.2	106
4. Franco Harris	13	2,949	12,120	4.1	91
5. Eric Dickerson	8	2,616	11,903	4.6	86
6. John Riggins	14	2,916	11,352	3.9	104
7. O. J. Simpson	11	2,404	11,236	4.7	61
8. Ottis Anderson	12	2,499	10,101	4.0	80
9. Earl Campbell	8	2,187	9,407	4.3	74
10. Jim Taylor	10	1,941	8,597	4.4	83
11. Joe Perry	14	1,737	8,378	4.8	53
12. Larry Csonka	11	1,891	8,081	4.3	64
13. Marcus Allen	9	1.960	7,957	4.1	75
14. Gerald Riggs	9	1,911	7,940	4.2	58
15. Freeman McNeil	10	1,704	7,604	4.5	36
16. Mike Pruitt	11	1,844	7,378	4.0	51
17. James Brooks	10	1,515	7,347	4.8	47
18. Leroy Kelly	10	1,727	7,274	4.2	74
19. George Rogers	7	1,692	7,176	4.2	54
20. Roger Craig	8	1,686	7,064	4.2	50

ALL-TIME
LEADING PASSERS

Joe Montana, Goerge Rose/NFL Photos.

	Yrs.	Att.	Comp.	Yards	TD	Int.	Rating
1. Joe Montana	12	4,579	2,914	34,998	242	123	93.4
2. Dan Marino	8	4,181	2,480	31,416	241	136	88.5
3. Boomer Esiason	7	2,687	1,520	21,381	150	98	85.8
Jim Kelly	5	2,088	1,251	15,730	105	72	85.8
5. Roger Staubach	11	2,958	1,685	22,700	153	109	83.4
6. Neil Lomax	8	3,153	1,817	22,771	136	90	82.7
7. Len Dawson	19	3,741	2,136	28,711	239	183	82.6
Sonny Jurgensen	18	4,262	2,433	32,224	255	189	82.6
9. Dave Krieg	11	3,291	1,909	24,052	184	136	82.3
10. Jim Everett	5	2,038	1,154	15,345	101	73	82.2
Ken O'Brien	9	2,878	1,697	20,444	109	78	82.2
12. Ken Anderson	16	4,475	2,654	32,838	197	160	81.9
13. Danny White	13	2,950	1,761	21,959	155	132	81.7
14. Bart Starr	16	3,149	1,808	24,718	152	138	80.5
15. Fran Tarkenton	18	6,467	3,686	47,003	342	266	80.4
16. Bernie Kosar	6	2,363	1,364	16,450	85	62	80.3
17. Dan Fouts	15	5,604	3,297	43,040	254	242	80.2
18. Warren Moon	7	3,025	1,701	22,989	134	112	79.9
19. Tony Eason	8	1,564	911	11,142	61	51	79.7
20. Jim McMahon	9	1,840	1,056	13,398	77	66	79.3

ALL-TIME
LEADING RECEIVERS

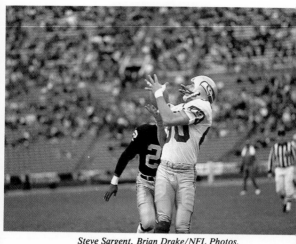

Steve Sargent, Brian Drake/NFL Photos.

		Yrs.	No.	Yards	Avg.	TD
1.	Steve Largent	14	819	13,089	16.0	100
2.	Charlie Joiner	18	750	12,146	16.2	65
3.	Art Monk	11	730	9,935	13.6	52
4.	Ozzie Newsome	13	662	7,980	12.1	47
5.	Charley Taylor	13	649	9,110	14.0	79
6.	James Lofton	13	642	11,963	18.6	61
7.	Don Maynard	15	633	11,834	18.7	88
8.	Raymond Berry	13	631	9,275	14.7	68
9.	Harold Carmichael	14	590	8,985	15.2	79
10.	Fred Biletnikoff	14	589	8,974	15.2	76
11.	Harold Jackson	16	579	10,372	17.9	76
12.	Lionel Taylor	10	567	7,195	12.7	45
13.	Wes Chandler	11	559	8,966	16.0	56
14.	Stanley Morgan	14	557	10,716	19.2	72
15.	J. T. Smith	13	544	6,974	12.8	35
16.	Lance Alworth	11	542	10,266	18.9	85
17.	Kellen Winslow	9	541	6,741	12.5	45
18.	John Stallworth	14	537	8,723	16.2	63
19.	Roy Green	12	522	8,496	16.3	66
20.	Bobby Mitchell	11	521	7,954	15.3	65

ALL-TIME
LEADING SCORERS

George Blanda, Malcolm Emmons/NFL Photos.

		Yrs.	TD	PAT	FG	Total
1.	George Blanda	26	9	943	335	2,002
2.	Jan Stenerud	19	0	580	373	1,699
3.	Jim Turner	16	1	521	304	1,439
4.	Mark Moseley	16	0	482	300	1,382
5.	Jim Bakken	17	0	534	282	1,380
6.	Fred Cox	15	0	519	282	1,365
7.	Pat Leahy	17	0	528	278	1,362
8.	Lou Groza	17	1	641	234	1,349
9.	Chris Bahr	14	0	490	241	1,213
10.	Nick Lowery	12	0	375	259	1,152
11.	Gino Cappelletti*	11	42	350	176	1,130
12.	Ray Wersching	15	0	456	222	1,122
13.	Don Cockcroft	13	0	432	216	1,080
14.	Garo Yepremian	14	0	444	210	1,074
15.	Jim Breech	12	0	459	201	1,062
16.	Bruce Gossett	11	0	374	219	1,031
17.	Eddie Murray	11	0	341	225	1,016
18.	Sam Baker	15	2	428	179	977
19.	Matt Bahr	12	0	378	199	975
20.	Rafael Septien	10	0	420	180	960

* Includes four two-point conversions

ANNUAL
RUSHING LEADERS

Year	Player, Team	Att.	Yards	Avg.	TD
1932	**Cliff Battles, Boston**	148	576	3.9	3
1933	Jim Musick, Boston	173	809	4.7	5
1934	**Beattie Feathers, Chi. Bears**	101	1,004	9.9	8
1935	Doug Russell, Chi. Cardinals	140	499	3.6	0
1936	**Alphonse (Tuffy) Leemans, NY Giants**	206	830	4.0	2
1937	Cliff Battles, Washington	216	874	4.0	5
1938	**Byron (Whizzer) White, Pittsburgh**	152	567	3.7	4
1939	**Bill Osmanski, Chi. Bears**	121	699	5.8	7
1940	Byron (Whizzer) White, Detroit	146	514	3.5	5
1941	Clarence (Pug) Manders, Brooklyn	111	486	4.4	5
1942	**Bill Dudley, Pittsburgh**	162	696	4.3	5
1943	**Bill Paschal, NY Giants**	147	572	3.9	10
1944	Bill Paschal, NY Giants	196	737	3.8	9
1945	Steve Van Buren, Philadelphia	143	832	5.8	15
1946	Bill Dudley, Pittsburgh	146	604	4.1	3
1947	Steve Van Buren, Philadelphia	217	1,008	4.6	13
1948	Steve Van Buren, Philadelphia	201	945	4.7	10
1949	Steve Van Buren, Philadelphia	263	1,146	4.4	11
1950	**Marion Motley, Cleveland**	140	810	5.8	3
1951	Eddie Price, NY Giants	271	971	3.6	7
1952	Dan Towler, LA Rams	156	894	5.7	10
1953	Joe Perry, San Francisco	192	1,018	5.3	10
1954	Joe Perry, San Francisco	173	1,049	6.1	8
1955	**Alan Ameche, Baltimore**	213	961	4.5	9
1956	Rich Casares, Chi. Bears	234	1,126	4.8	12
1957	**Jim Brown, Cleveland**	202	942	4.7	9
1958	Jim Brown, Cleveland	257	1,527	5.9	17
1959	Jim Brown, Cleveland	290	1,329	4.6	14
1960	Jim Brown, Cleveland, NFL	215	1,257	5.8	9
	Abner Haynes, Dallas Texans, AFL	157	875	5.6	9
1961	Jim Brown, Cleveland, NFL	305	1,408	4.6	8
	Billy Cannon, Houston, AFL	200	948	4.7	6
1962	Jim Taylor, Green Bay, NFL	272	1,474	5.4	19
	Cookie Gilchrist, Buffalo, AFL	214	1,096	5.1	13
1963	Jim Brown, Cleveland, NFL	291	1,863	6.4	12
	Clem Daniels, Oakland, AFL	215	1,099	5.1	3
1964	Jim Brown, Cleveland, NFL	280	1,446	5.1	7
	Cookie Gilchrist, Buffalo AFL	230	981	4.3	6
1965	Jim Brown, Cleveland, NFL	289	1,544	5.3	17
	Paul Lowe, San Diego, AFL	222	1,121	5.0	7
1966	Jim Nance, Boston, AFL	299	1,458	4.9	11
	Gale Sayers, Chi. Bears, NFL	229	1,231	5.4	8
1967	Jim Nance, Boston, AFL	269	1,216	4.5	7
	Leroy Kelly, Cleveland, NFL	235	1,205	5.1	11
1968	Leroy Kelly, Cleveland, NFL	248	1,239	5.0	16
	Paul Robinson, Cincinnati, AFL	238	1,023	4.3	8
1969	Gale Sayers, Chi. Bears, NFL	236	1,032	4.4	8
	Dickie Post, San Diego, AFL	182	873	4.8	6
1970	Larry Brown, Washington, NFC	237	1,125	4.7	5
	Floyd Little, Denver, AFC	209	901	4.3	3
1971	Floyd Little, Denver, AFC	284	1,133	4.0	6
	John Brockington, Green Bay, NFC	216	1,105	5.1	4

1972 O. J. Simpson, Buffalo, AFC	292	1,251	4.3	6
Larry Brown, Washington, NFC	285	1,216	4.3	8
1973 O. J. Simpson, Buffalo, AFC	332	2,003	6.0	12
John Brockington, Green Bay, NFC	265	1,144	4.3	3
1974 Otis Armstrong, Denver, AFC	263	1,407	5.3	9
Lawrence McCutcheon, LA Rams, NFC	236	1,109	4.7	3
1975 O. J. Simpson, Buffalo, AFC	329	1,817	5.5	16
Jim Otis, St. Louis, NFC	269	1,076	4.0	5
1976 O. J. Simpson, Buffalo, AFC	290	1,503	5.2	8
Walter Payton, Chi. Bears, NFC	311	1,390	4.5	13
1977 Walter Payton, Chi. Bears, NFC	339	1,852	5.5	14
Mark van Eeghen, Oakland, AFC	324	1,273	3.9	7
1978 Earl Campbell, Houston, AFC	302	1,450	4.8	13
Walter Payton, Chi. Bears, NFC	333	1,395	4.2	11
1979 Earl Campbell, Houston, AFC	368	1,697	4.6	19
Walter Payton, Chi. Bears, NFC	369	1,610	4.4	14
1980 Earl Campbell, Houston, AFC	373	1,934	5.2	13
Walter Payton, Chi. Bears, NFC	317	1,460	4.6	6
1981 George Rogers, New Orleans, NFC	378	1,674	4.4	13
Earl Campbell, Houston, AFC	361	1,376	3.9	10
1982 Freeman McNeil, NY Jets, AFC	151	786	5.2	6
Tony Dorsett, Dallas, NFC	177	745	4.2	5
1983 Eric Dickerson, LA Rams, NFC	390	1,808	4.6	18
Curt Warner, Seattle, AFC	335	1,449	4.3	13
1984 Eric Dickerson, LA Rams, NFC	379	2,105	5.6	14
Earnest Jackson, San Diego, AFC	296	1,179	4.0	8
1985 Marcus Allen, LA Raiders, AFC	380	1,759	4.6	11
Gerald Riggs, Atlanta, NFC	397	1,719	4.3	10
1986 Eric Dickerson, LA Rams, NFC	404	1,821	4.5	11
Curt Warner, Seattle, AFC	319	1,481	4.6	13
1987 Charles White, LA Rams, NFC	324	1,374	4.2	11
Eric Dickerson, Indianapolis, AFC	223	1,011	4.5	5
1988 Eric Dickerson, Indianapolis, AFC	388	1,659	4.3	14
Herschel Walker, Dallas, NFC	361	1,514	4.2	5
1989 Christian Okoye, Kansas City	370	1,480	4.0	12
Barry Sanders, Detroit, NFC	280	1,470	5.3	14
1990 Barry Sanders, Detroit, NFC	255	1,304	5.1	13
Thurman Thomas, Buffalo, AFC	271	1,297	4.8	11

Bold face – first year in league.

O J Simpson, Fred Kaplan/NFL Photos.

ANNUAL
PASSING LEADERS

Year Player, Team	Att.	Comp.	Yards	TD	Int.
1932 Arnie Herber, Green Bay	101	37	639	9	9
1933 **Harry Newman, NY Giants**	136	53	973	11	17
1934 Arnie Herber, Green Bay	115	42	799	8	12
1935 Ed Danowski, NY Giants	113	57	794	10	9
1936 Arnie Herber, Green Bay	173	77	1,239	11	13
1937 **Sammy Baugh, Washington**	171	81	1,127	8	14
1938 Ed Danowski, NY Giants	129	70	848	7	8
1939 **Parker Hall, Cleveland**	208	106	1,227	9	13
1940 Sammy Baugh, Washington	177	111	1,367	12	10
1941 Cecil Isbell, Green Bay	206	117	1,479	15	11
1942 Cecil Isbell, Green Bay	268	146	2,021	24	14
1943 Sammy Baugh, Washington	239	133	1,754	23	19
1944 Frank Filchock, Washington	147	84	1,139	13	9
1945 Sammy Baugh, Washington	182	128	1,669	11	4
Sid Luckman, Chi. Bears	217	117	1,725	14	10
1946 Bob Waterfield, LA Rams	251	127	1,747	18	17
1947 Sammy Baugh, Washington	354	210	2,938	25	15
1948 Tommy Thompson, Philadelphia	246	141	1,965	25	11
1949 Sammy Baugh, Washington	255	145	1,903	18	14
1950 Norm Van Broclin, LA Rams	233	127	2,061	18	14
1951 Bob Waterfield, LA Rams	176	88	1,566	13	10
1952 Norm Van Brocklin, LA Rams	205	113	1,736	14	17
1953 Otto Graham, Cleveland	258	167	2,722	11	9
1954 Norm Van Brocklin, LA Rams	260	139	2,637	13	21
1955 Otto Graham, Cleveland	185	98	1,721	15	8
1956 Ed Brown, Chi. Bears	168	96	1,667	11	12
1957 Tommy O'Connell, Cleveland	110	63	1,229	9	8
1958 Eddie LeBaron, Washington	145	79	1,365	11	10
1959 Charlie Conerly, NY Giants	194	113	1,706	14	4
1960 Milt Plum, Cleveland, NFL	250	151	2,297	21	5
Jack Kemp, LA Chargers, AFL	406	211	3,018	20	25
1961 George Blanda, Houston, AFL	362	187	3,330	36	22
Milt Plum, Cleveland, NFL	302	177	2,416	18	10
1962 Len Dawson, Dallas Texans, AFL	310	189	2,759	29	17
Bart Starr, Green Bay, NFL	285	178	2,438	12	9
1963 Y. A. Tittle, NY Giants, NFL	367	221	3,145	36	14
Tobin Rote, San Diego, AFL	286	170	2,510	20	17
1964 Len Dawson, Kansas City, AFL	354	199	2,879	30	18
Bart Starr, Green Bay, NFL	272	163	2,144	15	4
1965 Rudy Bukich, Chi. Bears, NFL	312	176	2,641	20	9
John Hadt, San Diego, AFL	348	174	2,798	20	21
1966 Bart Starr, Green Bay, NFL	251	156	2,257	14	3
Len Dawson, Kansas City, AFL	284	159	2,527	26	10
1967 Sonny Jurgensen, Washington, NFL	508	288	3,747	31	16
Daryle Lamonica, Oakland, AFL	425	220	3,228	30	20
1968 Len Dawson, Kansas City, AFL	224	131	2,109	17	9
Earl Morrall, Baltimore, NFL	317	182	2,909	26	17
1969 Sonny Jurgensen, Washington, NFL	442	274	3,102	22	15
Greg Cook, Cincinnati, AFL	197	106	1,854	15	11
1970 John Brodie, San Francisco, NFC	378	223	2,941	24	10
Daryle Lamonica, Oakland, AFC	356	179	2,516	22	15
1971 Roger Staubach, Dallas, NFC	211	126	1,882	15	4
Bob Griese, Miami, AFC	263	145	2,089	19	9

1972	Norm Snead, NY Giants, NFC	325	196	2,307	17	12
	Earl Morrall, Miami, AFC	150	83	1,360	11	7
1973	Roger Staubach, Dallas, NFC	286	179	2,428	23	15
	Ken Stabler, Oakland, AFC	260	163	1,997	14	10
1974	Ken Anderson, Cincinnati, AFC	328	213	2,667	18	10
	Sonny Jurgensen, Washington, NFC	167	107	1,185	11	5
1975	Ken Anderson, Cincinnati, AFC	377	228	3,169	21	11
	Fran Tarkenton, Minnesota, NFC	425	273	2,994	25	13
1976	Ken Stabler, Oakland, AFC	291	194	2,737	27	17
	James Harris, LA Rams, NFC	158	91	1,460	8	6
1977	Bob Griese, Miami, AFC	307	180	2,252	22	13
	Roger Staubach, Dallas, NFC	361	210	2,620	18	9
1978	Roger Staubach, Dallas, NFC	413	231	3,190	25	16
	Terry Bradshaw, Pittsburgh, AFC	368	207	2,915	28	20
1979	Roger Staubach, Dallas, NFC	461	267	3,586	27	11
	Dan Fouts, San Diego, AFC	530	332	4,082	24	24
1980	Brian Sipe, Cleveland, AFC	554	337	4,132	30	14
	Ron Jaworski, Philadelphia, NFC	451	257	3,529	27	12
1981	Ken Anderson, Cincinnati, AFC	479	300	3,753	29	10
	Joe Montana, San Francisco, NFC	488	311	3,565	19	12
1982	Ken Anderson, Cincinnati, AFC	309	218	2,495	12	9
	Joe Theismann, Washington, NFC	252	161	2,033	13	9
1983	Steve Bartkowski, Atlanta, NFC	432	274	3,167	22	5
	Dan Marino, Miami, AFC	296	173	2,210	20	6
1984	Dan Marino, Miami, AFC	564	362	5,084	48	17
	Joe Montana, San Francisco, NFC	432	279	3,630	28	10
1985	Ken O'Brien, NY Jets, AFC	488	297	3,888	25	8
	Joe Montana, San Francisco, NFC	494	303	3,653	27	13
1986	Tommy Kramer, Minnesota, NFC	372	208	3,000	24	10
	Dan Marino, Miami, AFC	623	378	4,746	44	23
1987	Joe Montana, San Francisco, NFC	398	266	3,054	31	13
	Bernie Kosar, Cleveland, AFC	389	241	3,033	22	9
1988	Boomer Esiason, Cincinnati, AFC	388	223	3,572	28	14
	Wade Wilson, Minnesota, NFC	332	204	2,746	15	9
1989	Joe Montana, San Francisco, NFC	386	271	3,521	26	8
	Boomer Esiason, Cincinnati, AFC	455	258	3,525	28	11
1990	Jim Kelly, Buffalo, AFC	346	219	2,829	24	9
	Phil Simms, NY Giants, NFC	311	184	2,284	15	4

Bold face – first year in league.

Roger Staubach, Rod Hanna/NFL Photos.

ANNUAL
RECEIVING LEADERS

Year Player, Team	No.	Yards	Avg.	TD
1932 Ray Flaherty, NY Giants	21	350	16.7	3
1933 John (Shipwreck) Kelly, Brooklyn	22	246	11.2	3
1934 Joe Carter, Philadelphia	16	238	14.9	4
Morris (Red) Badgro, NY Giants	16	206	12.9	1
1935 **Tod Goodwin, NY Giants**	26	432	16.6	4
1936 Don Hutson, Green Bay	34	536	15.8	8
1937 Don Hutson, Green Bay	41	552	13.5	7
1938 Gaynell Tinsley, Chi. Cardinals	41	516	12.6	1
1939 Don Hutson, Green Bay	34	846	24.9	6
1940 **Don Looney, Philadelphia**	58	707	12.2	4
1941 Don Hutson, Green Bay	58	738	12.7	10
1942 Don Hutson, Green Bay	74	1,211	16.4	17
1943 Don Hutson, Green Bay	47	776	16.5	11
1944 Don Hutson, Green Bay	58	866	14.9	9
1945 Don Hutson, Green Bay	47	834	17.7	9
1946 Jim Benton, LA Rams	63	981	15.6	6
1947 Jim Keane, Chi. Bears	64	910	14.2	10
1948 **Tom Fears, LA Rams**	51	698	13.7	4
1949 Tom Fears, LA Rams	77	1,013	13.2	9
1950 Tom Fears, LA Rams	84	1,116	13.3	7
1951 Elroy (Crazylegs) Hirsch, LA Rams	66	1,495	22.7	17
1952 Mac Speedie, Cleveland	62	911	14.7	5
1953 Pete Pihos, Philadelphia	63	1,049	16.7	10
1954 Pete Pihos, Philadelphia	60	872	14.5	10
Billy Wilson, San Francisco	60	830	13.8	5
1955 Pete Pihos, Philadelphia	62	864	13.9	7
1956 Billy Wilson, San Francisco	60	889	14.8	5
1957 Billy Wilson, San Francisco	52	757	14.6	6
1958 Raymond Berry, Baltimore	56	794	14.2	9
Pete Retzlaff, Philadelphia	56	766	13.7	2
1959 Raymond Berry, Baltimore	66	959	14.5	14
1960 Lionel Taylor, Denver, AFL	92	1,235	13.4	12
Raymond Berry, Baltimore, NFL	74	1,298	17.5	10
1961 Lionel Taylor, Denver, AFL	100	1,176	11.8	4
Jim (Red) Phillips, LA Rams, NLF	78	1,092	14.0	5
1962 Lionel Taylor, Denver, AFL	77	908	11.8	4
Bobby Mitchell, Washington, NFL	72	1,384	19.2	11
1963 Lionel Taylor, Denver, AFL	78	1,101	14.1	10
Bobby Joe Conrad, St. Louis, NFL	73	967	13.2	10
1964 Charley Hennigan, Houston, AFL	101	1,546	15.3	8
Johnny Morris, Chi. Bears, NFL	93	1,200	12.9	10
1965 Lionel Taylor, Denver, AFL	85	1,131	13.3	6
Dave Parks, San Francisco, NFL	80	1,344	16.8	12
1966 Lance Alworth, San Diego, AFL	73	1,383	18.9	13
Charley Taylor, Washington, NFL	72	1,119	15.5	12
1967 George Sauer, NY Jets, AFL	75	1,189	15.9	6
Charley Taylor, Washington, NFL	70	990	14.1	9
1968 Clifton McNeil, San Francisco, NFL	71	994	14.0	7
Lance Alworth, San Diego, AFL	68	1,312	19.3	10
1969 Dan Abramowicz, New Orleans, NFL	73	1,015	13.9	7
Lance Alworth, San Diego, AFL	64	1,003	15.7	4
1970 Dick Gordon, Chi. Bears, NFC	71	1,026	14.5	13
Marlin Briscoe, Buffalo, AFC	57	1,036	18.2	8

1971 Fred Biletnikoff, Oakland, AFC	61	929	15.2	9
Bob Tucker, NY Giants, NFC	59	791	13.4	4
1972 Harold Jackson, Philadelphia, NFC	62	1,048	16.9	4
Fred Biletnikoff, Oakland, AFC	58	802	13.8	7
1973 Harold Carmichael, Philadelphia, NFC	67	1,116	16.7	9
Fred Willis, Houston, AFC	57	371	6.5	1
1974 Lydell Mitchell, Baltimore, AFC	72	544	7.6	2
Charle Young, Philadelphia, NFC	63	696	11.0	3
1975 Chuck Foreman, Minnesota, NFC	73	691	9.5	9
Reggie, Rucker, Cleveland, AFC	60	770	12.8	3
1976 MacArthur Lane, Kansas City, AFC	66	686	10.4	1
Drew Pearson, Dallas, NFC	58	806	13.9	6
1977 Lydell Mitchell, Baltimore, AFC	71	620	8.7	4
Ahmad Rashad, Minnesota, NFC	51	681	13.4	2
1978 Rickey Young, Minnesota, NFC	88	704	8.0	5
Steve Largent, Seattle, AFC	71	1,168	16.5	8
1979 Joe Washington, Baltimore, AFC	82	750	9.1	3
Ahmad Rashad, Minnesota, NFC	80	1,156	14.5	9
1980 Kellen Winslow, San Diego, AFC	89	1,290	14.5	9
Earl Cooper, San Francisco, NFC	83	567	6.8	4
1981 Kellen Winslow, San Diego, AFC	88	1,075	12.2	10
Dwight Clark, San Francisco, NFC	85	1,105	13.0	4
1982 Dwight Clark, San Francisco, NFC	60	913	12.2	5
Kellen Winslow, San Diego, AFC	54	721	13.4	6
1983 Todd Christensen, LA Raiders, AFC	92	1,247	13.6	12
Roy Green, St. Louis, NFC	78	1,227	15.7	14
Charlie Brown, Washington, NFC	78	1,225	15.7	8
Earnest Gray, NY Giants, NFC	78	1,139	14.6	5
1984 Art Monk, Washington, NFC	106	1,372	12.9	7
Ozzie Newsome, Cleveland, AFC	89	1,001	11.2	5
1985 Roger Craig, San Francisco, NFC	92	1,016	11.0	6
Lionel James, San Diego, AFC	86	1,027	11.9	6
1986 Todd Christensen, LA Raiders, AFC	95	1,153	12.1	8
Jerry Rice, San Francisco, NFC	86	1,570	18.3	15
1987 J. T. Smith, St. Louis, NFC	91	1,117	12.3	8
Al Toon, NY Jets, AFC	68	976	14.4	5
1988 Al Toon, NY Jets, AFC	93	1,067	11.5	5
Henry Ellard, LA Rams, NFC	86	1,414	16.4	10
1989 Sterling Sharpe, Green Bay, NFC	90	1,423	15.8	12
Andre Reed, Buffalo, AFC	88	1,312	14.9	9
1990 Jerry Rice, San Francisco, NFC	100	1,502	15.0	13
Haywood Jeffires, Houston, AFL	74	1,048	14.2	8
Drew Hill, Houston, AFC	74	1,019	13.8	5

Bold face – first year in league.

Lance Alworth, NFL Photos.

ANNUAL
SCORING LEADERS

Year Player, Team	TD	FG	PAT	TP
1932 Earl (Dutch) Clark, Portsmouth	6	3	10	55
1933 Ken Strong, NY Giants	6	5	13	64
Glenn Presnell, Portsmouth	6	6	10	64
1934 Jack Manders, Chi. Bears	3	10	31	79
1935 Earl (Dutch) Clark, Detroit	6	1	16	55
1936 Earl (Dutch) Clark, Detroit	7	4	19	73
1937 Jack Manders, Chi. Bears	5	8	15	69
1938 Clarke Hinkle, Green Bay	7	3	7	58
1939 Andy Farkas, Washington	11	0	2	68
1940 Don Hutson, Green Bay	7	0	15	57
1941 Don Hutson, Green Bay	12	1	20	95
1942 Don Hutson, Green Bay	17	1	33	138
1943 Don Hutson, Green Bay	12	3	36	117
1944 Don Hutson, Green Bay	9	0	31	85
1945 Steve Van Buren, Philadelphia	18	0	2	110
1946 Ted Fritsch, Green Bay	10	9	13	100
1947 Pat Harder, Chi. Cardinals	7	7	39	102
1948 Pat Harder, Chi. Cardinals	6	7	53	110
1949 Pat Harder, Chi. Cardinals	8	3	45	102
Gene Roberts, NY Giants	17	0	0	102
1950 Doak Walker, Detroit	11	8	38	128
1951 Elroy (Crazylegs) Hirsch, LA Rams	17	0	0	102
1952 Gordy Soltau, San Francisco	7	6	34	94
1953 Gordy Soltau, San Francisco	6	10	48	114
1954 Bobby Walston, Philadelphia	11	4	36	114
1955 Doak Walker, Detroit	7	9	27	96
1956 Bobby Layne, Detroit	5	12	33	99
1957 Sam Baker, Washington	1	14	29	77
Lou Groza, Cleveland	0	15	32	77
1958 Jim Brown, Cleveland	18	0	0	108
1959 Paul Hornung, Green Bay	7	7	31	94
1960 Paul Hornung, Green Bay, NFL	15	15	41	176
Gene Mingo, Denver, AFL	6	18	33	123
1961 Gino Cappelletti, Boston, AFL	8	17	48	147
Paul Hornung, Green Bay, NFL	10	15	41	146
1962 Gene Mingo, Denver, AFL	4	27	32	137
Jim Taylor, Green Bay, NFL	19	0	0	114
1963 Gino Cappelletti, Boston, AFL	2	22	35	113
Don Chandler, NY Giants, NFL	0	18	52	106
1964 Gino Cappelletti, Boston, AFL	7	25	36	155
Lenny Moore, Baltimore, NFL	20	0	0	120
1965 Gale Sayers, Chi. Bears, NFL	22	0	0	132
Gino Cappelletti, Boston, AFL	0	17	27	132
1966 Gino Cappelletti, Boston, AFL	6	16	35	119
Bruce Gossett, LA Rams, NFL	0	28	29	113
1967 Jim Bakken St. Louis, NFL	0	27	36	117
George Blanda, Oakland, AFL	0	20	56	116
1968 Jim Turner, NY Jets, AFL	0	34	43	145
Leroy Kelly, Cleveland, NFL	20	0	0	120
1969 Jim Turner, NY Jets, AFL	0	32	33	129
Fred Cox, Minnesota, NFL	0	26	43	121
1970 Fred Cox, Minnesota, NFC	0	30	35	125
Jan Stenerud, Kansas City, AFC	0	30	26	116

1971	Garo Yepremian, Miami, AFC	0	28	33	117
	Curt Knight, Washington, NFC	0	29	27	114
1972	**Chester Marcol, Green Bay, NFC**	0	33	29	128
	Bobby Howfield, NY Jets, AFC	0	27	40	121
1973	David Ray, LA Rams, NFC	0	30	40	130
	Roy Gerela, Pittsburgh, AFC	0	29	36	123
1974	Chester Marcol, Green Bay, NFC	0	25	19	94
	Roy Gerela, Pittsburgh, AFC	0	20	33	93
1975	O. J. Simpson, Buffalo, AFC	23	0	0	138
	Chuck Foreman, Minnesota, NFC	22	0	0	132
1976	Toni Linhart, Baltimore, AFC	0	20	49	109
	Mark Moseley, Washington, NFC	0	22	31	97
1977	Errol Mann, Oakland, AFC	0	20	39	99
	Walter Payton, Chi. Bears, NFC	16	0	0	96
1978	**Frank Corral, LA Rams, NFC**	0	29	31	118
	Pat Leahy, NY Jets, AFC	0	22	41	107
1979	John Smith, New England, AFC	0	23	46	115
	Mark Moseley, Washington, NFC	0	25	39	114
1980	John Smith, New England, AFC	0	26	51	129
	Ed Murray, Detroit, NFC	0	27	35	116
1981	Ed Murray, Detroit, NFC	0	25	46	121
	Rafael Septien, Dallas, NFC	0	27	40	121
	Jim Breech, Cincinnati, AFC	0	22	49	115
	Nick Lowery, Kansas City, AFC	0	26	37	115
1982	**Marcus Allen, LA Raiders, AFC**	14	0	0	84
	Wendell Tyler, LA Rams, NFC	13	0	0	78
1983	Mark Moseley, Washington, NFC	0	33	62	161
	Gary Anderson, Pittsburgh, AFC	0	27	38	119
1984	Ray Wersching, San Francisco, NFC	0	25	56	131
	Gary Anderson, Pittsburgh, AFC	0	24	45	117
1985	**Kevin Butler, Chi. Bears, NFC**	0	31	51	144
	Gary Anderson, Pittsburgh, AFC	0	33	40	139
1986	Tony Franklin, New England, AFC	0	32	44	140
	Kevin Butler, Chi. Bears NFC	0	28	36	120
1987	Jerry Rice, San Francisco, NFC	23	0	0	138
	Jim Breech, Cincinnati, AFC	0	24	25	97
1988	Scott Norwood, Buffalo, AFC	0	32	33	129
	Mike Cofer, San Francisco, NFC	0	27	40	121
1989	Mike Cofer, San Francisco, NFC	0	29	49	136
	David Treadwell, Denver, AFC	0	27	39	120
1990	Nick Lowery, Kansas City, AFC	0	34	37	139
	Chip Lohmiller, Washington, NFC	0	30	41	131

Bold face – first year in league.

THE RULES OF THE NFL

The following rules have been taken from the Digest of
Rules of the National Football League. They are not
complete, but do give the basics of the game.

DEFINITIONS

1. **Chucking**: Warding off an opponent who is in front of
   a defender by contacting him with a quick extension of
   arm or arms, followed by the return of arm(s) to a
   flexed position, thereby breaking the original contact.
2. **Clipping**: Throwing the body across the back of an
   opponent's leg or hitting him from the back below the
   waist while moving up from behind unless the
   opponent is a runner or the action is in close line play.
3. **Close Line Play**: The area between the positions
   normally occupied by the offensive tackles, extending
   three yards on each side of the line of scrimmage.
4. **Crackback**: Eligible receivers who take or move to a
   position more than two yards outside the tackle may
   not block an opponent below the waist if they then
   move back inside to block.
5. **Dead Ball**: Ball not in play.
6. **Double Foul**: A foul by each team during the same
   down.
7. **Down**: The period of action that starts when the ball is
   put in play and ends when it is dead.
8. **Encroachment**: When a player enters the neutral zone
   and makes *contact* with an opponent before the ball is
   snapped.
9. **Fair Catch**: An unhindered catch of a kick by a
   member of the receiving team who must raise one arm
   a full length above his head while the kick is in flight.
10. **Foul**: Any violation of a playing rule.
11. **Free Kick**: A kickoff, kick after a safety, or kick after a
    fair catch. It may be a placekick, dropkick, or punt,
    except a punt may *not* be used on a kickoff.
12. **Fumble**: The loss of possession of the ball.
13. **Game Clock**: Scoreboard game clock.
14. **Impetus**: The action of a player that gives momentum
    to the ball.
15. **Live Ball**: A ball legally free kicked or snapped. It
    continues in play until the down ends.
16. **Loose Ball**: A live ball not in possession of any player.
17. **Muff**: The touching of a loose ball by a player in an
    unsuccessful attempt to obtain possession.
18. **Neutral Zone**: The space length of a ball between
    the two scrimmage lines. The offensive team and

defensive team must remain behind their end of the ball.

Exception: The offensive player who snaps the ball.

19. **Offside**: A player is offside when any part of his body is beyond his scrimmage or free kick line *when the ball is snapped*.

20. **Own Goal**: The goal a team is guarding.

21. **Play Clock**: 45/25 second clock.

22. **Pocket Area**: Applies from a point two yards outside of either offensive tackle and includes the tight end if he drops off the line of scrimmage to pass protect. Pocket extends longitudinally behind the line back to offensive team's own end line.

23. **Possession**: When a player controls the ball throughout the act of *clearly* touching both feet, or any other part of his body other than his hand(s), to the ground inbounds.

24. **Punt**: A kick made when a player drops the ball and kicks it while it is in flight.

25. **Safety**: The situation in which the ball is dead on or behind a team's own goal if the *impetus* comes from a player on that team. Two points are scored for the opposing team.

26. **Shift**: The movement of two or more offensive players at the same time before the snap.

27. **Striking**: The act of swinging, clubbing, or propelling the arm or forearm in contacting an opponent.

28. **Sudden Death**: The continuation of a tied game into sudden death overtime in which the team scoring first (by safety, field goal, or touchdown) wins.

29. **Touchback**: When a ball is dead on or behind a team's own goal line, provided the impetus came from an opponent and provided it is not a touchdown or a missed field goal.

30. **Touchdown**: When any part of the ball, legally in possession of a player inbounds, is on, above, or over the opponent's goal line, provided it is not a touchback.

31. **Unsportsmanlike Conduct**: Any act contrary to the generally understood principles of sportsmanship.

SUMMARY OF PENALTIES
Automatic First Down

1. Awarded to offensive team of all *defensive fouls* with these exceptions:
   (a) Offside.
   (b) Encroachment.
   (c) Delay of game.
   (d) Illegal substitution.
   (e) Excessive time out(s).

    (f) Incidental grasp of facemask.
    (g) Prolonged, excessive or premeditated celebrations by individual players or groups of players.
    (h) Running into the kicker.

Loss of Down (No yardage)
1. Second forward pass *behind* the line.
2. Forward pass strikes ground, goal post, or crossbar.
3. Forward pass goes out of bounds.
4. Forward pass is first touched by eligible receiver who has gone out of bounds and returned.
5. Forward pass touches or is caught by an ineligible receiver on or behind line.
6. Forward pass thrown from behind line of scrimmage after ball once crossed the line.

Five Yards
1. Crawling.
2. Defensive holding or illegal use of hands (automatic first down).
3. Delay of game.
4. Encroachment.
5. Too many time outs.
6. False start.
7. Illegal formation.
8. Illegal shift.
9. Illegal motion.
10. Illegal substitution.
11. First onside kickoff out of bounds between goal lines and not touched.
12. invalid fair catch signal.
13. More than 11 players on the field at snap for either team.
14. Less than seven men on offensive line at snap.
15. Offside.
16. Failure to pause one second after shift or huddle.
17. Running into kicker.
18. More than one man in motion at snap.
19. Grasping facemask of opponent.
20. Player out of bounds at snap.
21. Ineligible member(s) of kicking team going beyond line of scrimmage before ball is kicked.
22. Illegal return.
23. Failure to report change of eligibility.
24. Prolonged, excessive or premeditated celebrations by individual players or groups of players.
25. Loss of team time out(s) or five-yard penalty on the defense for excessive crowd noise.

10 Yards
1. Offensive pass interference.
2. Ineligible player downfield during passing down.

3. Holding, illegal use of hands, arms or body by offense.
4. Tripping by a member of either team.
5. Helping the runner.
6. Illegal batting or punching a loose ball.
7. Deliberately kicking a loose ball.

15 Yards

1. Chop block.
2. Clipping below the waist.
3. Fair catch interference.
4. Illegal crackback block by offense.
5. Piling on (automatic first down).
6. Roughing the kicker (automatic first down).
7. Roughing the passer (automatic first down).
8. Twisting, turning, or pulling an opponent by the facemask.
9. Unnecessary roughness.
10. Unsportsmanlike conduct.
11. Delay of game at start of either half.
12. Illegal blocking below the waist.
13. A tackler using his helmet to butt, spear, or ram an opponent.
14. Any player who uses the top of his helmet unnecessarily.
15. A punter, placekicker or holder who simulates being roughed by a defensive player.
16. A defender who takes a running start from beyond the line of scrimmage in an attempt to block a field goal or point after touchdown.

Five Yards and Loss of Down

1. Forward pass thrown from *beyond* line of scrimmage.

10 Yards and Loss of Down

1. Intentional grounding of forward pass (safety if passer is in own end zone). If foul occurs more than 10 yards behind line, play results in loss of down at spot of foul.

15 Yards and Loss of Coin Toss Option

1. Team's late arrival on the field prior to scheduled kickoff.

15 Yards (and disqualification if flagrant)

1. Striking opponent with fist.
2. Kicking or kneeing opponent.
3. Striking opponent on head or neck with forearm, elbow, or hands whether or not the initial contact is made below the neck area.
4. Roughing kicker.
5. Roughing passer.
6. Malicious unnecessary roughness.
7. Unsportsmanlike conduct.

8. Palpably unfair act (Distance penalty determined by the Referee after consultation with other officials.)

15 Yards and Automatic Disqualification
    1. Using a helmet that is not worn as a weapon.

Suspension From Game
    1. Illegal equipment. (Player may return after one down when legally equipped.)

Touchdown
    1. When Referee determines a palpably unfair act deprived a team of a touchdown. (Example: Player comes off bench and tackles runner apparently en route to touchdown.)

FIELD
1. Sidelines and end lines are *out of bounds*. The *goal line* is *actually in the end zone*. A player with the ball in his possession scores when the ball is *on, above,* or *over* the goal line.
2. The field is rimmed by a white border, a minimum six feet wide, along the sidelines. All of this is *out of bounds*.
3. The hashmarks (inbound lines) are 70 feet, 9 inches from each sideline.
4. Goal posts must be single-standard type, offset from the *end* line and painted bright gold. The goal posts must be 18 feet, 6 inches wide and the top face of the crossbar must be 10 feet above the ground. Vertical posts extend at least 30 feet above the crossbar. A ribbon 4 inches by 42 inches long is to be attached to the top of each post. The actual goal is the plane extending indefinitely above the crossbar and between the *outer* edges of the posts.
5. The field is 360 feet long and 160 feet wide. The end zones are 30 feet deep. The line used in try-for-point plays is two yards out from the goal line.

COIN TOSS
1. The toss of coin will take place within three minutes of kickoff in center of field. The toss will be called by the visiting captain. The winner may choose one of two privileges and the loser gets the other:
    (a) Receive or kick
    (b) Goal his team will defend
2. Immediately prior to the start of the second half, the captains of both teams must inform the officials of their respective choices. The loser of the original coin toss gets first choice.

TIMING

1. The stadium game clock is official. In case it stops or is operating incorrectly, the *Line Judge* takes over the official timing on the field.
2. Each period is 15 minutes. The intermission between the periods is two minutes. Halftime is 12 minutes, unless otherwise specified.
3. On charged team time outs, the Field Judge starts watch and blows whistle after 1 minute 50 seconds, unless television does not utilize the time for commercial. In this case the length of the time out is reduced to 40 seconds.
4. Referee may allow two minutes for injured player and three minutes for equipment repair.
5. Each team is allowed three time outs each half.
6. Time between plays will be 45 seconds from the end of a given play until the snap of the ball for the next play, or a 25-second interval after certain administrative stoppages and game delays.
7. Clock will start running when ball is snapped following all changes of team possession.
8. With the exception of the last two minutes of the first half and the last five minutes of the second half, the game clock will be restarted following a kickoff return, a player going out of bounds, or after all declined penalties on the Referee's ready singal.
9. Consecutive team time outs can be taken by opposing teams but the length of the second time out will be reduced to 40 seconds.
10. When, in the judgement of the Referee, the level of crowd noise prevents the offense from hearing its signals, he can institute a series of procedures which can result in a loss of team time outs or a five-yard penalty against the defensive team.

SUDDEN DEATH

1. The sudden death system of determining the winner shall prevail when score is tied at the end of the regulation playing time of *all NFL games*. The team scoring first during overtime play shall be the winner and the game automatically ends upon any score (by safety, field goal, or touchdown) or when a score is awarded by Referee for a palpably unfair act.

TRY-FOR-POINT

1. After a touchdown, the scoring team is allowed a try-for-point during one scrimmage down. The ball may be spotted anywhere between the inbounds lines, two or more yards from the goal line. The successful conversion counts one point, whether by run, kick, or pass.

2. The *defensive team never can score* on a try-for-point. As soon as defense get possession, or kick is blocked, ball is dead.

3. Any distance penalty for fouls committed by the defense that prevent the try from being attempted can be enforced on the succeeding kickoff. Any foul committed on a successful try will result in a distance penalty being assessed on the ensuing kickoff.

4. Only the fumbling player may advance a fumble during a try-for-point.

PLAYERS-SUBSTITUTIONS

1. Each team is permitted 11 men on the field at the snap.

2. Unlimited substitution is permitted. However, players may enter the field only when the ball is dead. Players who have been substituted for are not permitted to linger on the field. Such lingering will be interpreted as unsportsmanlike conduct.

3. Players leaving the game must be out of bounds *on their own side*, clearing the field *between the end lines*, before a snap or free kick. If player crosses end line leaving field, it is delay of game (five-yard penalty).

4. Substitutes who remain in the game must move onto the field as far as the inside of the field numerals before moving to a wide position.

KICKOFF

1. The kickoff shall be the kicking team's 35 yard line at the start of each half and after a field goal and try-for-point. A kickoff is one type of free kick.

2. Either a one-, two-, or three-inch tee may be used (no tee permitted for field goal or try-for-point plays). The ball is put in play by a placekick or dropkick.

3. If kickoff clears the opponent's goal posts it is *not a field goal*.

4. A kickoff is illegal unless it travels 10 yards OR is touched by the *receiving* team. Once the ball is touched by the receiving team it is a free ball. Receivers may recover and advance. Kicking team may recover but *NOT* advance *UNLESS* receiver had possession and lost the ball.

5. When a kickoff goes out of bounds between the goal lines without being touched by the receiving team, the ball belongs to the receivers 30 yards from the spot of the kick or at the out-of-bounds spot unless the ball went out-of-bounds the first time an onside kick was attempted. In this case the kicking team is to be penalized five yards and the ball must be kicked again.

6. When a kickoff goes out of bounds between the goal lines and is *touched last by* receiving team, it is receiver's ball at out-of-bounds spot.

FREE KICK

1. In addition to a kickoff, the other free kicks are a kick after a safety and a kick after a fair catch. In both cases, a dropkick, placekick, or punt may be used (a punt may *not* be used on a kickoff).
2. On a free kick *after a fair catch*, captain of receiving team has the option to put ball in play by punt, dropkick, or placekick *without* a tee, or by snap. If the placekick or dropkick goes between the uprights a field goal is scored.
3. On a free kick after a safety, the team scored upon puts ball in play by a punt, dropkick, or placekick without tee. *No score* can be made on a free kick following a safety, even if a series of penalties places team in position.

FIELD GOAL

1. All field goals attempted and missed from scrimmage line beyond the 20 yard line will result in the defensive team taking possession of the ball at the scrimmage line. On any field goal attempted and missed from scrimmage line inside the 20 yard line, ball will revert to defensive team at the 20 yard line.

SAFETY

1. The important factor in a safety is impetus. Two points are scored for the opposing team when the ball is dead on or behind a team's own goal line *if the impetus came from a player on that team*.

Examples of Safety:

(a) Blocked punt goes out of kicking team's end zone. Impetus was provided by punting team. The block only changes direction of ball, no impetus.
(b) Ball carrier retreats from field of play *into his own end zone* and is downed. Ball carrier provides impetus.
(c) Offensive team commits a foul and spot of enforcement is *behind its own goal line*.
(d) Player on receiving team muffs punt and, trying to get ball, forces or illegally kicks it into end zone where he or a teammate recovers. He has given new impetus to the ball.

POSITION OF PLAYERS AT SNAP

1. Offensive team must have *at least seven* players on line.
2. Offensive players, not on line, must be on at least one yard back at snap. (**Exception**: player who takes snap.)
3. No interior lineman may move after taking or simulating a three-point stance.

4. No player of either team may invade neutral zone before snap.

5. No player of offensive team may charge or move, after assuming set position, in such manner as to lead defense to believe snap has started.

6. If a player changes his eligibility, the Referee must alert the defensive captain after player has reported to him.

7. All players of offensive team must be stationary at snap, except one back who may be in motion parallel to scrimmage line or backward (not forward).

8. After a shift or huddle all players on offensive team must come to an absolute stop *for at least one second* with no movement of hands, feet, head, or swaying of body.

9. Quarterbacks can be called for a false start penalty (five yards) if their actions are judged to be an obvious attempt to draw an opponent offside.

USE OF HANDS, ARMS, AND BODY

1. No player on offense may assist a runner except by blocking for him. There shall be no interlocking interference.

2. A runner may ward off opponents with his hands and arms but no other player on offense may use hands or arms to obstruct an opponent by grasping with hands, pushing, or encircling any part of his body during a block. Hands (open or closed) can be thrust forward to initially contact an opponent on or outside the opponent's frame, but the blocker must work to bring his hands on or inside the frame.

3. Hands cannot be thrust forward *above* the frame to contact an opponent on the neck, face or head.

4. A *defensive* player may not tackle or hold an opponent other than a runner. Otherwise, he may use his hands, arms or body only:
   (a) To defend or protect himself against an obstructing opponent.
   (b) To push or pull opponent out of the way on line of scrimmage.
   (c) In actual attempt to get at or tackle runner.
   (d) To push or pull opponent out of the way in a legal attempt to recover a loose ball.
   (e) During a legal block on an opponent who is not an eligible pass receiver.
   (f) When legally blocking an eligible pass receiver above the waist.

5. A defensive player must not contact an opponent above the shoulders with the palm of his hand *except* to ward him off on the line. This exception is permitted

only if it is not a repeated act against the same opponent during any one contact. In all other cases the palms may be used on head, neck, or face only to ward off or push an opponent in legal attempt to get at the ball.

6. Any offensive player who pretends to possess the ball or to whom a teammate pretends to give the ball may be tackled provided he is *crossing* his scrimmage line between the ends of a normal tight offensive line.

7. An offensive player who lines up more than two yards outside his own tackle or a player who, at the snap, is in a backfield position and subsequently takes a position more than two yards outside a tackle may not clip an opponent anywhere nor may he contact an opponent below the waist if the blocker is moving toward the ball and if contact is made within an area five yards on either side of the line.

8. A player of either team may block at any time provided it is not pass interference, fair catch interference, or unnecessary roughness.

FORWARD PASS

1. A forward pass may be touched or caught by any eligible receiver. All members of the defensive team are eligible. Eligible receivers on the offensive team are players on either end of line (other than center, guard, or tackle) or players at least one yard behind the line at the snap. A T-formation quarterback is *not* eligible to receive a forward pass during a play from scrimmage. **Exception:** T-formation quarterback becomes eligible if pass is previously touched by an eligible receiver.

2. An offensive team may make only *one* forward pass during each play from scrimmage (Loss of down).

3. The passer must be behind his line of scrimmage (Loss of down and five yards, enforced from the spot of pass).

4. Any eligible offensive player may catch a forward pass. If a pass is touched by one offensive player and touched or caught by a second eligible offensive player, pass completion is legal. Further, all offensive players become eligible once a pass is touched by an eligible receiver or any defensive player.

5. The rules concerning a forward pass and ineligible receivers:
   (a) If ball is touched *accidentally* by an ineligible receiver on *or behind his line*: loss of down.
   (b) If ineligible receiver is illegally downfield: loss of 10 yards.
   (c) If touched or caught (intentionally or accidentally) by ineligible receiver *beyond* the line: loss of 10 yards or loss of down.

6. The player who first controls and continues to maintain control of a pass will be awarded the ball even though his opponent later establishes joint control of the ball.
7. Any forward pass becomes incomplete and ball is dead if:
   (a) Pass hits the ground or goes out of bounds.
   (b) Hits the goal post or the crossbar of either team.
   (c) Is caught by offensive player after touching ineligible receiver.
   (d) An illegal pass is caught by the passer.
8. A forward pass is complete when a receiver clearly touches the ground with *both feet* inbounds while in *possession* of the ball. If a receiver would have landed inbounds with both feet but is carried or pushed out of bounds while maintaining possession of the ball, pass is complete at the out-of-bounds spot.
9. If an eligible receiver goes out of bounds accidentally or is forced out by a defender and returns to catch a pass, the play is regarded as a pass caught out of bounds. (Loss of down, no yardage.)
10. On a *fourth down* pass – when the offensive team is *inside* the *opposition's 20 yard line* – an incomplete pass results in a loss of down at the line of scrimmage.
11. If a personal foul is committed by the *defense prior* to the completion of a pass, the penalty is 15 yards from the spot where ball becomes dead.
12. If a personal foul is committed by the *offense prior* to the completion of a pass, the penalty is 15 yards from the previous line of scrimmage.

INTENTIONAL GROUNDING OF FORWARD PASS

1. Intentional grounding of a forward pass is a foul: loss of down and 10 yards from previous spot if passer is in the field of play or loss of down at the spot of the foul if it occurs more than 10 yards behind the line or safety if passer is in his own end zone when ball is released.
2. It is considered intentional grounding of a forward pass when the ball strikes the ground after the passer throws, tosses, or lobs the ball to prevent a loss of yards by his team.
3. It is not intentional grounding when the defensive rushers have not put sufficient pressure on the passer to prevent him, for strategic purposes, from throwing the ball downfield in a natural and effective motion even though there is no apparent chance of completion.

PROTECTION OF PASSER

1. By interpretation, a pass begins when the passer – with possession of ball – starts to bring his hand forward. If

ball strikes ground after his action has begun, play is ruled an incomplete pass. If passer loses control of ball prior to his bringing his hand forward, play is ruled a fumble.

2. No defensive player may run into a passer of a legal forward pass after the ball has left his hand (15 yards). The Referee must determine whether opponent had a *reasonable chance to stop his momentum* during an attempt to block the pass or tackle the passer while he still had the ball.

PASS INTERFERENCE

1. There shall be no interference with a forward pass thrown from behind the line. The restriction for the *passing team* starts *with the snap*. The restriction on the *defensive team* starts *when the ball leaves the passer's hand*. Both restrictions *end when the ball is touched by anyone*.

2. The penalty for *defensive* pass interference is an automatic first down at the spot of the foul. If interference is in the end zone, it is first down for the offense on the defense's 1 yard line. If previous spot was inside the defense's 1 yard line, penalty is half the distance to the goal line.

3. The penalty for *offensive* pass interference is 10 yards from the previous spot.

4. It is pass interference by either team when any player movement beyond the offensive line significantly hinders the progress of an eligible player or such player's opportunity to catch the ball during a legal forward pass. When players are competing for position to make a play on the ball, any contact by hands, arms or body shall be considered incidental unless prohibited. Prohibited conduct shall be when a player physically restricts or impedes the opponent in such a manner that is *visually evident* and *materially affects* the opponent's opportunity to gain position or retain his position to catch the ball. If a player has gained position, he shall not be considered to have impeded or restricted his opponent in a prohibited manner if all of his actions are a bona fide effort to go and catch the ball. Provided an eligible player is not interfered with in such a manner, the following exceptions to pass interference will prevail:

   (a) If neither player is looking for the ball and there is incidental contact in the act of moving to the ball that does not materially affect the route of an eligible player, there is no interference. If there is any question whether the incidental contact materially affects the route, the ruling shall be no interference.

Note: Inadvertent tripping is not a foul in this situation.

(b) Any eligible player looking for and intent on playing the ball who initiates contact, however severe, while attempting to move to the spot of completion or interception will not be called for interference.

(c) Any eligible player who makes contact, however severe, with one or more eligible players while looking for and making a genuine attempt to catch or bat a reachable ball, will not be called for interference.

(d) It must be remembered that defensive players have as much right to the ball as offensive eligible receivers.

(e) Pass interference by the defense is not to be called when the forward pass is clearly uncatchable.

(f) Note: There is no defensive pass interference behind the line.

BACKWARD PASS

1. Any pass not forward is regarded as a backward pass or lateral. A pass parallel to the line is a backward pass. A runner may pass backward at any time. *Any player on either team* may catch the pass or recover the ball after it touches the ground.

2. A backward pass that strikes the ground can be recovered and advanced by offensive team.

3. A backward pass that strikes the ground can be *recovered* but *cannot be advanced* by the *defensive team*.

4. A backward pass *caught in the air* can be *advanced* by the *defensive team*.

FUMBLE

1. The distinction between a *fumble* and a *muff* should be kept in mind in considering rules about fumbles. A *fumble* is the *loss of possession* of the ball. A muff is the touching of a loose ball by a player in an *unsuccessful attempt to obtain possession*.

2. A fumble may be advanced by any player on either team regardless of whether recovered before or after ball hits the ground.

3. A fumble that goes forward and out of bounds will return to the fumbling team at the spot of the fumble unless the ball goes out of bounds in the opponent's end zone. In this case, the defensive team is to take possession at the spot of the fumble.

4. If an offensive player fumbles anywhere on the field during a fourth down play, or if a player fumbles on

any down after the two-minute warning in a half, only the fumbling player is permitted to recover and/or advance the ball. If recovered by any other offensive player, the ball is dead at the spot of the fumble unless it is recovered behind the spot of the fumble. In that case, ball is dead at spot of recovery. Any defensive player may recover and/or advance any fumble.

KICKS FROM SCRIMMAGE

1. Any punt or missed field goal that touches a goal post is dead.
2. During a kick from scrimmage, *only the end men*, as eligible receivers on the line of scrimmage at the time of the snap, are permitted to go beyond the line before the ball is kicked.
   Exception: An eligible receiver who, at the snap, is aligned or in motion behind the line and more than one yard outside the end man on his side of the line, clearly making him the outside receiver, REPLACES that end man as the player eligible to go downfield after the snap. All other members of the kicking team must remain at the line of scrimmage until the ball has been kicked.
3. Any punt that is blocked and does *not* cross the line of scrimmage can be recovered and advanced by either team. However, if offensive team recovers it must make the yardage necessary for its first down to retain possession if punt was on fourth down.
4. The kicking team may never advance its own kick even though legal recovery is made beyond the line of scrimmage. Possession only.
5. A member of the receiving team may not run into or rough a kicker who kicks from behind his line unless contact is:
   (a) Incidental to and *after* he had touched ball in flight.
   (b) Caused by kicker's own motions.
   (c) Occurs during a quick kick, or a kick made after a run, or after kicker recovers a loose ball. Ball is loose when kicker muffs snap or snap hits ground.
   (d) Defender is blocked into kicker.
   The penalty for *running* into the kicker is 5 yards. For *roughing* the kicker: 15 yards, an automatic first down and disqualification if flagrant.
6. If a member of the kicking team attempting to down the ball on or inside opponent's 5 yard line carries the ball into the end zone, it is a touchback.
7. Fouls during a punt are enforced from the previous spot (line of scrimmage).
   Exception: Illegal touching, illegal fair catch, invalid

    fair catch signal, and fouls by the receiving team during loose ball after ball is kicked.

8. While the ball is in the air or rolling on the ground following a punt or field goal attempt and receiving team commits a foul before gaining possession, receiving team will retain possession and will be penalized for its foul.

9. It will be illegal for a defensive player to jump or stand on any player, or be picked up by a teammate or to use a hand or hands on a teammate to gain additional height in an attempt to block a kick (Penalty 15 yards, unsportsmanlike conduct).

10. A punted ball remains a kicked ball until it is declared dead or in possession of either team.

11. Any member of the punting team may *down* the ball anywhere in the field of play. However, it is *illegal touching* (Official's time out and receiver's ball at spot of illegal touching). This foul does *not* offset any foul by receivers during the down.

12. Defensive team may advance all kicks from scrimmage (including unsuccessful field goal) whether or not ball crosses defensive team's goal line. Rules pertaining to kicks from scrimmage apply until defensive team gains possession.

FAIR CATCH

1. The member of the receiving team must raise one arm a full length above his head and wave it from side to side while kick is in flight. (Failure to give proper sign: receivers' ball five yards behind spot of signal.)
   Note: It is legal for the receiver to shield his eyes from the sun by raising one hand no higher than the helmet.

2. No opponent may interfere with the fair catcher, the ball, or his path to the ball. Penalty: 15 yards from spot of foul and fair catch is awarded.

3. A player who signals for a fair catch is *not* required to catch the ball. However, if a player signals for a fair catch, he may not block or initiate contact with any player on the kicking team *until the ball touches a player. Penalty: snap 15 yards behind spot of foul.*

4. If ball hits ground or is touched by members of kicking team in flight, fair catch signals is off and all rules for a kicked ball apply.

5. Any *undue advance* by a fair catch receiver is delay of game. No specific distance is specified for 'undue advance' as ball is dead at spot of catch. If player comes to a reasonable stop, no penalty. For violation, five yards.

6. If time expires while ball is in play and a fair catch is awarded, receiving team may choose to extend the

period with one free kick down. However, placekicker may *not* use tee.

FOUL ON LAST PLAY OF HALF OR GAME

1. On a foul by *defense* on last play of half or game, the *down is replayed* if penalty is accepted.
2. On a foul by the *offense* on last play of half or game, the *down is not replayed* and the play in which the foul is committed is nullified.
   Exception: Fair catch interference, foul following change of possession, illegal touching. *No score by offense counts.*
3. On *double foul* on last play of half or game, *down is replayed*.

SPOT OF ENFORCEMENT OF FOUL

1. There are four basic spots at which a penalty for a foul is enforced:
   (a) Spot of foul: The spot where the foul is committed.
   (b) Previous spot: The spot where the ball was put in play.
   (c) Spot of snap, pass, fumble, return kick, or free kick: The spot where the act connected with the foul occurred.
   (d) Succeeding spot: The spot where the ball next would be put in play if no distance penalty were to be enforced.
   Exception: If foul occurs after a touchdown and before the whistle for a try-for-point, succeeding spot is spot of next kickoff.
2. All fouls committed by *offensive* team *behind* the line of scrimmage and in the field of play shall be penalized from the *previous spot*.
3. When spot of enforcement for fouls involving defensive holding or illegal use of hands by the defense is behind the line of scrimmage, any penalty yardage to be assessed on that play shall be measured from the line if the foul occurred beyond the line.

DOUBLE FOUL

1. If there is a double foul *during* a down in which there is a change of possession, the team last gaining possession may keep the ball unless its foul was committed prior to the change of possession.
2. If double foul occurs *after* a change of possession, the defensive team retains the ball at the spot of its foul or dead ball spot.
3. If one of the fouls of a double foul involves disqualification, that player must be removed, but no

penalty yardage is to be assessed.
4. If the kickers foul during a punt before possession changes and the receivers foul after possession changes, penalties will be offset and the down is replayed.

PENALTY ENFORCED ON FOLLOWING KICKOFF

1. When a team scores by touchdown, field goal, extra point, or safety and either team commits a personal foul, unsportsmanlike conduct, or obvious unfair act during the down, the penalty will be assessed on the following kickoff.

THE NFL DRAFT

The format of the NFL draft has changed many times since
the brainchild of former NFL Commissioner and club
owner Bert Bell was accepted by the team owners on 19
May 1935. Bell's idea was to help the weaker teams by
allowing them first choice of the top college players. Teams
would draft in inverse order of their finish, with the league
champion selecting last, regardless of its record. Prior to
that time, players had been able to sign with any club.
Open signing tended to make the strong stronger.

The initial draft was held 8 February 1936 and consisted
of nine rounds. The next year, the draft had 10 rounds, and
in 1939 it increased to 20 rounds. During World War II, the
draft was expanded to 30 rounds, the assumption being
many of those drafted also would be drafted by the Armed
Forces.

From 1947 to 1958, the bonus pick rule was in effect.
Each year one team received the first pick in the draft,
selected by lottery. Each team was eligible only once.

When the AFL was founded prior to the 1960 season,
the two leagues began drafting many of the same players.
Part of the merger agreement between the AFL and NFL
was to hold a combined draft, which started in 1967 and
was shortened to 17 rounds. The draft was further reduced
to 12 rounds in 1977; the same year it was moved to late
April or May.

NUMBER-ONE DRAFT CHOICES

Season	Team	Player	Position	College
1936	Philadelphia	Jay Berwanter	HB	Chicago
1937	Philadelphia	San Francisco	FB	Nebraska
1938	Cleveland	Corbett Davis	FB	Indiana
1939	Chicago Cardinals	Ki Aldrich	C	Texas Christian
1940	Chicago Cardinals	George Cafego	HB	Tennessee
1941	Chicago Bears	Tom Harmon	HB	Michigan
1942	Pittsburgh	Bill Dudley	HB	Virginia
1943	Detroit	Frank Sinkwich	HB	Georgia
1944	Boston	Angelo Bertelli	QB	Notre Dame
1945	Chicago Cardinals	Charley Trippi	HB	Georgia
1946	Boston	Frank Dancewicz	QB	Notre Dame
1947	Chicago Bears	Bob Fenimore	HB	Oklahoma A&M
1948	Washington	Harry Gilmer	QB	Alabama
1949	Philadelphia	Chuck Bednarik	C	Pennsylvania
1950	Detroit	Leon Hart	E	Notre Dame
1951	New York Giants	Kyle Rote	HB	Southern Methodist
1952	Los Angeles	Bill Wade	QB	Vanderbilt
1953	San Francisco	Harry Babcock	E	Georgia
1954	Cleveland	Bobby Garrett	QB	Stanford
1955	Baltimore	George Shaw	QB	Oregon
1956	Pittsburgh	Gary Glick	DB	Colorado A&M
1957	Green Bay	Paul Hornung	HB	Notre Dame
1958	Chicago Cardinals	King Hill	QB	Rice
1959	Green Bay	Randy Duncan	QB	Iowa
1960	Los Angeles	Billy Cannon	RB	Louisiana State

(AFL had no formal first pick)

Season	Team	Player	Position	College
1961	Buffalo (AFL)	Ken Rice	G	Auburn
	Minnesota	Tommy Mason	RB	Tulane
1962	Oakland (AFL)	Roman Gabirel	QB	North Carolina State
	Washington	Ernie Davis	RB	Syracuse
1963	Kansas City (AFL)	Buck Buchanan	DT	Grambling
	Los Angeles	Terry Baker	QB	Oregon State
1964	Boston (AFL)	Jack Concannon	QB	Boston College
	San Francisco	Dave Parks	E	Texas Tech
1965	Houston (AFL)	Lawrence Elkins	E	Baylor
	New York Giants	Tucker Frederickson	RB	Auburn
1966	Miami (AFL)	Jim Grabowski	RB	Illinois
	Atlanta	Tommy Nobis	LB	Texas
1967	Baltimore	Bubba Smith	DT	Michigan State
1968	Minnesota	Ron Yary	T	Southern California
1969	Buffalo	O. J. Simpson	RB	Southern California
1970	Pittsburgh	Terry Bradshaw	QB	Louisiana Tech
1971	New England	Jim Plunkett	QB	Stanford
1972	Buffalo	Walt Patulski	DE	Notre Dame
1973	Houston	John Matuszak	DE	Tampa
1974	Dallas	Ed Jones	DE	Tennessee State
1975	Atlanta	Steve Bartkowski	QB	California
1976	Tampa Bay	Lee Roy Selmon	DE	Oklahoma
1977	Tampa Bay	Ricky Bell	RB	Southern California
1978	Houston	Earl Campbell	RB	Texas
1979	Buffalo	Tom Cousineau	LB	Ohio State
1980	Detroit	Billy Sims	RB	Oklahoma
1981	New Orleans	George Rogers	RB	South Carolina
1982	New England	Kenneth Sims	DT	Texas
1983	Baltimore	John Elway	QB	Stanford
1984	New England	Irving Fryar	WR	Nebraska
1985	Buffalo	Bruce Smith	DE	Virginia Tech
1986	Tampa Bay	Bo Jackson	RB	Auburn
1987	Tampa Bay	Vinny Testaverde	QB	Miami
1988	Atlanta	Aundray Bruce	LB	Auburn
1989	Dallas	Troy Aikman	QB	UCLA
1990	Indianapolis	Jeff George	QB	Illinois
1991	Dallas	Russell Maryland	DT	Miami

INDEX